Robert Andrew Macfie

Colonial Questions Pressing for Immmediate Solution,

in the Interest of the Nation and the Empire

Robert Andrew Macfie

Colonial Questions Pressing for Immmediate Solution,
in the Interest of the Nation and the Empire

ISBN/EAN: 9783337153045

Printed in Europe, USA, Canada, Australia, Japan

Cover: Foto ©ninafisch / pixelio.de

More available books at **www.hansebooks.com**

COLONIAL QUESTIONS

PRESSING FOR IMMEDIATE SOLUTION,

IN THE INTEREST OF

THE NATION AND THE EMPIRE.

Papers and Letters

BY

R. A. MACFIE, M.P.,

MEMBER OF THE ROYAL COLONIAL INSTITUTE.

"IN THE MULTITUDE OF PEOPLE IS THE KING'S HONOUR; BUT IN THE WANT OF PEOPLE IS THE DESTRUCTION OF THE PRINCE."

"PORTAS INTRARE PATENTES;
PATIENTE COLONO
ARVA PREMI."

"THIS GREAT NATION, WITH BOUNDLESS COLONIES WHICH WOULD REWARD ENTERPRISE AND ABUNDANTLY YIELD THE FRUITS OF TOIL, YET STANDS BEFORE THE WORLD WITH THE SHAMEFUL AVOWAL THAT HER POVERTY AND HER CRIME INFLICT TAXATION UPON HER POPULATION TO THE EXTENT OF TWENTY MILLIONS A-YEAR."—*Prospectus of Workmen's Emigration Society.*

LONDON:
LONGMANS, GREEN, READER, AND DYER.
EDMONSTON & DOUGLAS, EDINBURGH.

[Price One Shilling.]   1871.   [Postage, Twopence.

I AM ANXIOUS THAT, WHILE THE QUEEN'S DOMINIONS ENJOY EVERYWHERE THE BLESSING OF TRANQUILLITY PROSPERITY, AND LOYALTY, THERE SHOULD BE INSTITUTED SUCH A CONSTITUTIONAL CONNEXION BETWEEN THE MOTHER COUNTRY AND THE COLONIES AS WILL CONSOLIDATE THE BRITISH EMPIRE, AND SUSTAIN ITS PATRIOTISM, STRENGTH, AND POWER.—*Candidate's Printed Address to Electors of Leith Burghs,* 1868.

(*From the "Leith Herald," September*, 1868.)

"I will proceed now to state my views on the great questions that occur to my mind, although, perhaps, they do not assume in the popular view all the importance I assign them. I will speak of the British Empire as a whole. I look upon the face of the globe, and I find this is the day of great Empires. We have near us the great Empire of France, and a little further distance away the newly-constituted great empire of Germany. We have beyond that the great Empire of Russia; and we have, more formidable still, the great nation of the United States of America. (Hear, hear.) Now, if the United Kingdom is to maintain its ground—to stand on an equal footing with these great Empires—I think we must not forget that it is necessary to maintain our magnitude also. We are possessed of vast territories, but, for good or for ill, these territories are widely scattered over various parts of the world. We are not so compact as any of these four Empires I have mentioned. Well, if we cannot be compact by being one great land, we may be compact by means of cordial unions between Britain and her Colonies. (Loud cheers.) The British people, as a nation, have done, I believe, most ample justice to the Colonists that have left our shores and settled in our valuable territories; but we have, as I apprehend, been too generous or too confiding. We have not stipulated, in return for the protection we afford them—for the powers we have conferred upon them—that these favours shall be at all reciprocated, by furnishing a fair quota of the men and part of the money that may be necessary for defence, and perhaps to fight the battles of the Empire. (Cheers.) Nay, we have been so extremely liberal that, whilst we have removed the protection in which they formerly revelled, we have allowed them to institute a new kind of protection injurious to ourselves. Their own manufactures they protect, and they exclude, by high duties, the manufactures of the Mother Country. (Hear, hear.) It appears to me the time has come when we ought to consolidate the British Empire, and unite this country and these Colonies by some system of federation, or some system of union, so that the great mass then will work together and act together, they and we finding the common fund of men and money requisite for Imperial purposes, and thus removing all prejudice that might exist in our minds against them. (Cheers.) Happily, this is a favourable time for seeking such a reform. All the Colonies are in a state of the most satisfactory contentment, with one exception—that exception is Nova Scotia, which has no prejudice against the Mother Country. . . . My mind now naturally turns to the great question of Emigration, for which these territories offer a most wide field. Now, I must at once say that I deplore the extent to which the ports of Leith and Liverpool are made the channel for banishing from our lands so many thousands of our fellow-countrymen—our most valuable fellow-subjects. (Hear, hear.) I believe, however desirable change of residence may be for the emigrant, that it is not required by over-population that any leave our own country. I believe that by an amendment of the land laws we could maintain on our soil, thriving and blessed under God, double the population that now occupies the acres of our country. (Loud cheers.) The calculation has lately been made as to what is the value of the article we bestow when we send a man abroad. Take the cost of production—the mother's care in his youth, his maintenance, his education, and his training in early life—and £100 would not pay the value of the gift we bestow on our Colonies when we send forth an able man.* Then that £100, itself a producer, is invested in such a way that it may bring forth twenty, sixty, or one hundredfold. Now, much as I value the connexion that subsists between the United Kingdom and the States of America, I tell you we are hurting ourselves deplorably in taking active measures to send away these most valuable workers. One distinction, I think, is drawn between the emigrant to the Colonies and the emigrant to the United States. The latter never returns. He becomes for ever, not merely expatriated, but the citizen of a foreign country. The former frequently comes back; and while he remains in the Colonies he feels that he is a British subject, and he maintains his loyal allegiance to the Crown of his country. (Cheers.) How much, then, ought we to prefer that our emigrants should flow in the direction of the Colonies, where they will be equally welcome as in America, and where they may soon become proprietors of land. That brings me back to the importance of uniting the Colonies to the Mother Country so thoroughly that we can still claim their services, and still reap the benefit of the emigrants' muscles and cordial good-will, and not lose their patriotism, for which I am sure they will become daily more remarkable." (Cheers.)— *Extract from Mr. Macfie's Address at Leith.*

---

* The productive value of a man may more truly and appreciatively be reckoned £500. The reader will excuse such a way of exhibiting a value that is *inestimable*. (See page 91.)

PREFATORY NOTE.

The Extracts which precede, and the Object in view, will, the writer trusts, justify publication of the Papers which follow, notwithstanding imperfection of style. In the language of the produce market, they are exposed all-faults.

Questions connected with the relation between the United Kingdom and the Colonies are now much better understood, and receive much more attention, than was the case even so late as two years ago. Hardly any of the published or spoken addresses at the last general election touched on them. If we do not misread "Hansard," the whole subject was ignored in both Houses of Parliament in the session of 1868-9. Not so last session. Still, the course taken by Government was regarded as not satisfactory by a growing number of members on both sides. The reign of absolute indifference is now past. Were it otherwise, recent movements in the Australian Colonies would constrain our earnest attention; prominent among which is the fact that a Royal Commission, or Select Committee, at Melbourne has, by a majority, proposed that the British Parliament should be asked to sanction some relationship to the Mother Country, or rather to the Sovereign only, that would entitle a contemplated Union to make treaties and be engaged in war, " as may to the Colonies seem wise and expedient"—that is, without regard to the interests or the will of the rest of the Empire; or, plainly, in practical disconnexion therefrom.

The writer does not attribute the highest importance to the recent speech at Boston of General Butler, nor to the still later Presidential Address. But the threat these hold out of non-intercourse, foreshadows more or less remote probabilities, and indicate belief, fostered, one is afraid, by observation of ugly facts, that undue concern for the maintenance of trade and manufactures is a snare and a danger to Britain. Why should the British people longer so exclusively cultivate and depend on manufactures and trade, as to give ground and encouragement for inimical or hostile treatment? Are we not disregarding the manifest interests of the United Kingdom and of the whole Empire,—and the opportunities, the duties, and the career, which possession of invaluable and almost boundless territories of our own, where the British and Irish peasant, more prosperous than at home, would be gratefully loyal to our Queen and institutions, unequivocally present and press upon us,—when we abstain from considering the best means of welding the Colonies to one another and to ourselves as a UNITAS FRATRUM? Why, in these times, when the air all around is surcharged with electricity that may bring the pealing and pelting thunderclouds of war over our heads, do we neglect the ready and noble means which union with such a hardy and attached population as the Colonial would insure for the raising of additional forces and acquiring additional power of resistance? Is there not confidence in the Colonists that they will discharge the duties, and fulfil zealously the responsibilities, that will devolve on them when admitted to their just and equal rights including in these a fair share of the government of that ancient and loyal Empire whose honour, and strength, and union they, like ourselves, fondly and proudly seek to maintain and promote?

To illustrate by fresh cases, is it reasonable, is it prudent, to part with any portion of the British territory—for instance, a naval station like the Gambia, which the Cape route, likely to become again our most reliable one to the East, renders, some tell us, invaluable—without consulting the Colonists, not even those whose trade with the Mother Country is conducted along its shore? Or to prosecute the great work of devising a naval and military system, and making and manning fortifications (that are demanded by threatenings, whose origin, ground, and motives, being imperial and national, are as much their concern as ours), without affording them the means and the satisfaction of jointly deliberating on, directing, and influencing the nature and extent of these defences, and the decision of such a question as peace or war?

Is the Empire to be bereft of its most populous and populable parts because the rulers of the United Kingdom have other cares to occupy their minds? Is no endeavour to be made to avert the evil? When will there be a more convenient season?

Success would be the crowning triumph of a Premier who knows what is due to the people. The nobles and the masses alike wait not without deep anxiety his action; continued non-action is predicable failure—foreseen partition of the Empire-trust.

To the Papers read before the Social Science Association are appended two letters on the same subject, and extracts from Dr. Lang's new Book in favour of Colonial Independence, and from the latest Report on Emigration. If the present *brochure* should reach that venerable gentleman's eye, may it lead him to consider whether the *via media* is not *tutissima*. Before leaping into the gulf of separation, whence there can be no harking back, why not " trust and try;"—trust the rest of the nation, which he professes to love much, and try if those are not in the right who said a nobler aspiration and a greater and better future than he aims at will be found in Independent Confederation?

It is *apropos* to add that a similar appeal may fairly be made to the statesmen at home who look with complacency on Separation. *First*, do they consider that if their ideas and anticipations should prove to be a mistake, and if consequently the greater Colonies are encouraged or allowed to go, there are not now any other unoccupied territories to be had on the globe for British colonization? *Secondly*, even if they are *not* too much afraid of the difficulty of holding Canada in the event of troubles with the United States (of whose principle and practice they think disparagingly), why speak and act so as to generate disloyal and bad feeling in Africa and Australia?

Probably, when the subject of Federation is proposed, our Irish neighbours may take advantage of the occasion to delineate their scheme for giving back to that chronically complaining country a Legislature of her own. Well, the people of England and Scotland, though they at present fail to see its practicability and promise of good, will look at the scheme without adverse prejudice, and would be happy if the consequence prove advantageous to her or to her and them.

The reader will find a passing allusion to our too little observed deficiency in *national spirit*. It is a significant fact, and the *fons et origo malorum*, that, whereas there has long been a United *Kingdom*, and in spite of our harmony and unity of feeling, we are, not only at home, but over the world, anything but a *united people*. We call ourselves English, Scotch, and Irish, but not *British*, although, indeed, this last word, in spite of its inappropriateness, the children of the great Islands are obliged to use, for want of any other, when they mean to indicate that common nationality which exists, and which ought now to be cherished and made more palpable and pervasive, more endearing and binding and stimulating. We should feel, and speak, and act *everywhere* as *one people*. Nationalism is in the ascendant abroad. On the Continent it is wisely cultivated and trained as a matter of State policy. We, Briton-Irish or Anglo-Celts, have an indisputable and fertile ground whereon to plant and uprear ours. "Germania," or the German race, has surprised mankind by the vigour and number and effects of its new national songs. Has the Poet Laureate, whose epic has so nobly prepared the public mind, struck the first note in Court circles? How many popular muses will join in concert, and the inspiriting "peaceful notes prolong?"

ASHFIELD HALL,
    21st *December*, 1870.

CONTENTS.

NOTES ON COLONIAL AND IMPERIAL POLICY: *A Paper read before the Association for Promoting Social Science, at Newcastle-upon-Tyne*, 1870.

	PAGE
The Colonial Question not a Party one	1
Constitutional Changes are Required	1
Object to Promote Stability and Interest of Empire	1
What the "Empire" is	1
"The Mother Country"	1
The Celtic Element, and Service it renders	2
Queen and Parliament Act and Legislate for whole British Dominions	3
British Sway is Mild and Confiding	3
The Transfers of Invaluable Productive Lands	3
Those Transfers should have been under Conditions	3
Conditions were Implied	3
"Nation" comprehends all at Home and in Colonies	4
Facilities for Settlers an Imperial Concern	4
Emigration to Colonies, not Foreign Countries, the Nation's Interest	4
In Colonies Emigrants augment Nation's Wealth and Strength	4
Manufacturing and Trading Pre-eminence is Unstable	5
British Consumers far more Beneficial than Foreign	5
Manufacturing Prosperity depends on Increased Consumption or New Markets	5
Trade tends irrepressibly towards Increased Operations	5
Dead-locks and Crises inevitable in Commerce	6
Farming has no such Drawbacks	6
What is the Permanent Product of our Trading Ascendancy?	6
Statesmen neglect Agricultural Development	6
Agriculture would make Population overflow into Colonies	7
Causing remarkable Prosperity and Population	7
While Britain free from Dangerous Classes	7
Policy points to Land-Cultivation in Colonies	7
This would lead to Greater National Independence	8
And Complete Harmony between United Kingdom and Colonies	8
Grand Field for Reciprocative Supply and Demand	8
Formidable Danger of Persisting in Indifference	8

CONTENTS.

	PAGE
Aggrandizement of other Nations	9
Their Advantages not Superior to our Own	9
Concessions to Colonies Necessitate Progress in same Direction	9
Systematised Emigration a Boon Conferrible on Colonies	9
Population and Capital should be Diffused over the Empire	10
National Spirit must be Cherished	10
Other Nations show us an Example	10
The Colonial Office might be Re-Formed	10
Functions of Royalty and Nobility	11
Anciently the Nobles discharged Public Responsibilities	11
Division of Great Estates and Exchange of Lands for Colonial	12
Colonial Orders of Knighthood fall Short	12
Equality of Subjects must be Principle of British Rule	12
"Mother of Nations" an Objectionable Name	12
United Kingdom is a "Mother of States"	13
Rendering like Allegiance	13
Comparison of Colonies to Children Inapt	13
They and United Kindom are Brothers who are Partners	13
The Capital—viz., Lands—held for Behoof of Family or "Firm"	13
Self-Government now Enjoyed by Principal Colonies	14
They have Equal Interest with us in Good Government of Empire	14
From Participation in which they cannot longer be Excluded	14
Experience and Observation show their Participation Required	14
Business of Colonies at Home now Done Unsatisfactorily	15
More Sympathy and Leisure Required at Colonial Office	15
Representation in Parliament would not Serve	15
A Colonial Board	16
Representation in the British Cabinet Insufficient	16
An Imperial Cabinet or Council solves Difficulties	16
Only other Alternative is Disruption of Empire	17
Parliamentary Negligence and Careless Expressions of Statesmen	17
Letter from *Canada* showing Apprehensions of Severance	18
"Annexationists"	18
Abandonment of *Canadian* Fortresses	18
Promised Assistance in case of War	18
Congress at *Melbourne*, and tendency to Independence	19
Independence compatible with Confederation	19
Lessons from the Growth of other Nations	19
A Nation's Power Proportionate to its Population	20
Tenure of *India* stands connected with Retention of Colonies	20
Isolation of Portions of Empire is Strength as well as Weakness	20
A Strong Power is usually at Peace with other Nations	20
Advantage of Harbours and Depôts in Colonies	21
Cosmopolitanism of Free-trade must not be Abused	21
The Feelings of Colonies must be Regarded	21

	PAGE
Foreign and Colonial Trade	22
Advantage of Possessing Unoccupied Territories.	23
Growing Strength of a United Empire	24
Good Understanding with the United States	24
Vision of Nearer Relations with United States.	25
Firm Resolution to Maintain Colonial Relations	26
Consultation with the Colonies.	26
Defences of the Empire	27
Cannot be Arranged by Correspondence	27
Council of the Empire	28
Feeling in the Colonies	28

THE UNITED KINGDOM AND THE COLONIES ONE AUTONOMIC
EMPIRE: *A Paper read before the Association for the Promotion
of Social Science at Bristol*, 1869 30

Comparative Strength of Great Nations	30
The Great Trust Committed to Britons	31
Agriculture *versus* Manufactures	32
Emigration not Pursued on Sound Principle	33
Concessions to Colonies have Conciliated	34
Their Equality with the United Kingdom Welcomed.	34
Amalgamation of Interests.	35
Value of British Connexion to the Colonies	35
The United Kingdom must Show itself Worthy.	35
The National Debt should be Reduced	36
Sufficient Defences must be Maintained	37
The Rights which the United Kingdom has in the Colonies	38
Responsibilities and Duties of the Peerage.	39
Advantage of Colonial Element in London.	40
Misuse of the Word "Imperial"	40

LETTER TO A PROMINENT MEMBER OF THE CABINET. 41

Evil of Deferring Consideration of the Colonial Question	41
The Recent Congress at *Melbourne*	42
Independence meant is Disintegration of the Empire.	42
Federation of the Empire	43
Our Position compared with that of Foreign Powers.	43
Implied Condition to Maintain Waste Lands for the Purposes of Emigration.	44
Proposal for a Convention of Delegates	44

LETTER TO THE TIMES 45

Extracts from *Melbourne* Newspaper.	45
Extracts from *Montreal* Newspaper	46
Dangerous Declarations by the Government	47
Regarded in light from the *Edinburgh Review*	48

CONTENTS.

	PAGE
Dr. Lang's New Book, " The Coming Event "	48
Deputations from the Colonies Proposed	49
EXTRACT FROM A NEW ZEALAND NEWSPAPER	49
Extract from Report of the *Victoria* Commission . . .	50
Remarks made by the *Pall Mall Gazette*	50
Mutual Affections of *Canada* and the Mother Country . .	50
Extract from the *British Columbia Gazette*	51
Very slight Recognition of the Mother Country	51
LETTER FROM CAPTAIN COLOMB ON COLONIAL DEFENCES .	52
Canadian Defences	53
Lines of Intercommunication by Sea	54
Strategic Points	54
Defences of whole Empire must be Considered Together . .	55
AUTHOR OF "FRIENDS IN COUNCIL" on Unification and Federation, and a Council	56
CLIPPINGS FROM DR. LANG'S NEW BOOK	57
Status quo of Colonial Question not Satisfactory . . .	57
Pleas in Favour of Independence	57
The Mother Country's Alleged Consent	58
The Object Dr. *Lang* has in View	58
The Inter-Colonial Conference in *Melbourne*	58
An Incorporating Union of Seven Provinces	59
Protectorate over *Fiji* hinges on Independence . . .	59
Talk about Annexation to United States or Germany . .	60
Dr. *Lang's* Definition of a Colony	60
Which are the British Colonies ?	61
The Object of Colonization	62
It is Britain's Duty to Colonize	62
General Ignorance on the Colonial Question	63
Bad System of Governing Colonies has Passed Away . .	63
They Aspire to be Nationalities	63
Improper Views on Allegiance to the QUEEN . . .	63
" The Colonies have Reached their Majority " . . .	34
Correction of a Common Misapprehension	64
The Views of Mr. *Wakefield* as to Love of England . .	65
United Kingdom does not wish to Dominate over Colonies .	65
Confederation	65
"The Empire is likely to be Dismembered " . . .	66
" The United Kingdom has been Ambitious and Proud " .	66
Unwarranted Expressions Emanating from the United Kingdom	66
British Public is not Prepared to Sanction a Disintegrative Policy	68
Grecian Colonization	68
And *Roman*	69

	PAGE
American Colonization	69
Favours Union rather than Disintegration	70
Manner of Dealing with Waste Lands by *United States*	71
A Quotation from *Grotius*	71
Dr. *Adam Smith* on the Relationship of Colonies	71
Dr. *Benjamin Franklin* on the same	72
Resolution of the *American Congress*	72
Opinion of *Jeremy Bentham*	72
Opinions of *Mr. Merivale* and *Mr. Carlyle*	73
Britain Alleged to have Received Compensation for Planting Colonies	73
A Great Mistake in the Author's Views	74
"Independence is Claimed Irrespectively of Compensation"	74
Mr. *Wakefield* again Referred to	74
"Colonial Interests must not be Compromised"	73
"United Kingdom is Hampered by its Heavy Debt."	75
Mr. *Wakefield's* View as to *Prestige* Controverted	75
Works of *Earl Grey* and *Sir George Lewis*	75
Advantages which Colonies Confer on the Mother Country	76
Those which Colonies Receive from the Mother Country	76
The Value of Trade with the Colonies	77
Sir *H. Parnell* Reckons Unwarrantably on same Trade after Separation	77
Alleged Advantage of the Separation of the *United States* questioned	77
"Emigration the Grand Question of the Day"	78
"Waste Lands Belonged to the Mother Country"	78
"It was a Mistake to Alienate Them"	78
Undue Flow towards the *United States*	79
Anti-Immigration League and Sentiment in *Australia*	79
There Ought to be a *Bonus* to attract Emigrants	79
Valuable Parliamentary Return on Waste Lands	80
Negotiations Regarding Australian Waste Lands and Emigration	80
Charge of Mismanagement by Unconditional Transfer	80
Australians would yet pay "Tribute" to Promote Emigration	81
The Act 18 and 19 Victoria, cap. 54	81
Lord Russell	81
Mr. Froude's Indignation at Transfer of Lands	82
How *Dr. Lang* Persuades the Colonists to seek Independence	82
Alleged Advantages to the United Kingdom and the Colonies	83
Great Britain must Dictate Terms when conceding Separation	83
Dr. Lang's too sanguine Expectation as to Australian Federation	84
The Abortive *London* Conference	84
Opinions of *Earl Grey* and *Duke of Manchester*	84
A Council to Supersede the Colonial Office	84

	PAGE
SPEECH OF LORD SANDON in Favour of Confederation of the Empire	85
Working Classes regarded Colonial Lands as their Birthright	85
Unity of the Empire should be earnestly watched over	85
Sir *Philip Wodehouse's* Misconception	86

REPORT OF THE EMIGRATION COMMISSIONERS:—

Classification of Emigrants in regard to Nationality	86
Increase of English and Scotch Emigrants	87
Emigration, 1869, from United Kingdom to *United States*	87
Emigration in Steamships	87
Mortality in Steamships	88
Total Emigration, 1847-69	88
Large Sum Contributed from Private Sources	88
Misappropriation of Emigration Fund in *South Australia*	88
Emigrants to *Canada* are largely Destined for United States	88
Revenue from Land, &c., in *New South Wales*	89
The same in *Queensland*	90
Table of Emigration in 1870	91
Money Estimate of the Annual Loss of so many Emigrants	91
Who also leave behind them Unliquidated Liability to National Debt	91
Americans find too ready Responses to their "Wilings Away"	92
PROCEEDINGS OF THE ROYAL COLONIAL INSTITUTE.—Mr. Westgarth on the Feelings and Position of the Colonies	93
EXTRACT OF A LETTER FROM CANADA	95
An Illustration and Warning from Glasgow	96
INDEX	97

IMPERIAL AND COLONIAL POLICY.

A PAPER READ BEFORE THE ASSOCIATION FOR THE PROMOTION OF SOCIAL SCIENCE, AT NEWCASTLE-UPON-TYNE, 1870.

The subject which I bring under your notice is, happily, not a party one. It is, undoubtedly, a field on which there has been some conflict of opinion; it may soon be a battle-ground on which parties, with opposing projects, will meet in earnest combat; but both sides will contend "in the Queen's name." The contest may be vehement, but it will be conducted with the ardour of loyalty to the same Crown, and with the aims of a common patriotism. Let us hope and strive that the public mind then may be found so enlightened and so leavened with sound principles, that the only issue to be tried shall be, what policy and what *constitutional changes* (for to these we may look forward) will most conduce to the stability, the prosperity, and the influence of the Empire.

What, I here ask, is "the British Empire"? Rather awkwardly, we have the Queen designated "Empress of India," and we speak of "the Indian Empire." But there are not *two* Empires under Her Most Gracious Majesty's sway. Still less are the British Islands, though in Royal Speeches and official language the expression may have been ventured, *the* Empire. No; these, Great Britain and Ireland, are "the United Kingdom," and "the Empire" includes, along with "the Mother Country," the Colonies and Dependencies thereto belonging.

The "Mother Country," I have said: it is an endearing name, and well expresses the regard and reverence in which the soil from which the Anglo-Saxon race have sprung, and to which our affections cling, is held by her many children scattered abroad. What a magic there is to Southrons and Hibernians in the names, "Old England!" "Ould Ireland!" If Caledonia, with her mountains and her floods, has no such adjectival prefix usually attached to her venerated names, it surely does not indicate want of feeling, but only undemonstrativeness, on the part of Sawnie and Donald. Pardon me, Donald *and Brother Pat*, for using the term "Anglo-Saxon." Perhaps the better designation is "Anglo-*Celt*," for we do not forget the several nationalities and races whose blood has been commingled in the vigorous and vivacious population of the realm. This intermixture inspires in our breasts through you a sentiment of kindred with the men of other European stocks, who have been absorbed or merged within our Colonies, or with whom, aliens dwelling in foreign countries, we are brought into relations by diplomacy and commerce.

None will question that the object—the true and noblest object—of British policy, in reference to the Colonies, is the stability, the prosperity, and the influence of the Empire, not of the United Kingdom only.

It would not be fair or generous for the British Cabinet or the Parliament of the United Kingdom to govern the Empire and frame its laws, with a view to home interests only or chiefly. The Queen is the

Queen, not of a part of the Empire, but of the whole. The Parliament rules and legislates for the Colonies, over which the Three Estates are by constitution supreme *pro bono publico* in the widest sense.

Certainly this sway has been exercised most mildly, and considerately, and confidingly. Think of the self-government that has been offered to the Colonies, and of our statesmen's abstinence from interference in their domestic concerns, and of the rareness with which control has been exercised and demands made or even explanations asked hence. These communities know and feel that they are free, like and along with ourselves who are at home.

Think, further, of the transfers made, without equivalent and without condition, of millions on millions of productive lands. That was implicit confidence indeed!

It might have been wiser and better for all parties if these lands had either not been transferred, or had been transferred upon some distinct condition that they should be promptly let or sold, or turned to account in the ways most likely to promote the welfare of the whole people, and not merely of the persons who have already settled or will settle there, and, in particular, that they should be as easily as possible obtainable by immigrants.

However that may be, two things are obvious—that the Government and Legislature of the Mother Country transferred these territories on an implied, though necessarily unexpressed, understanding that the Colonial connexion is indissoluble; and, further, that what the Mother Country, almost unsought and altogether without a price, gave, she relied on the Colonists being ready to dispose of in such a manner as to attract thither her surplus population; for this nation, which still realizes the blessing or command, " Be fruitful and multiply, and replenish the earth"—the *nation*, by which term we mean the whole people, wherever in the wide world located—had a right to expect this return.

It is not to the nation, especially not to the masses, a matter of indifference and unimportance whether unoccupied lands are available or unavailable on easy terms for settlers. If the terms are high and difficult to comply with, the greater nearness, compared with Africa or Australia, of the United States, the superiority of that country's climate, compared with the climate of Canada, and the facilities afforded in the States or in Southern America, will, as in the past, so, most surely, in the future, turn the stream of emigrants away from the destination which otherwise they would choose, and which we and they, on the strongest and most irrefragable grounds, prefer.

Every man who leaves our shores for the Colonies, there to farm, goes to increase the population, and the wealth, and the strength of the Empire. Every man who leaves for the United States is a subtraction from our numbers, and, *per contra*, becomes a producer of wealth and an accumulator of power for them instead of for ourselves. True, he will still be a consumer of British and Colonial wares, even on alien soil. He will be so, perhaps, for his life-time (in years of peace), but not to anything like the extent which could be predicated of him if he continued a British subject.

Beware of the conceit that the people of the United Kingdom, or the manufacturing and trading portions of us who export—a comparatively small section—will continue able for the future, as in the past, to undersell other countries from this as "the workshop for all the world." Act not on the assumption that there will be no serious obstruction to trade from wars or hostile tariffs. Besides: the tailor, cobbler, and grocer —for they and such like, and not the *employés* in huge factories, are the staple of our industrious non-agricultural population—will tell us they know too well by experience that every expatriation of a neighbour is, even during peace, their unmixed loss.

But, whether well or ill founded the assumption of perpetual superiority, or expectation of such perpetual commercial superiority as is looked for by many, it is abnegation of national independence, and courting national dangers, to act on it. Consider for a moment what, in the most favourable circumstances, is involved in "manufacturing for the world," and in the pursuit of manufacturing prosperity. According to the nature of things, in order to maintain such prosperity there must be either continual increase of consumption on the part of persons or peoples who are already customers, or else continual opening of new markets: for this reason, that every success and every improvement in mechanism leads to increase of operations and of output in existing establishments, and neighbours' observation of success, and the hiring off of clerks and partners who set up for themselves, lead, with the same certainty, to the formation of additional establishments, which in their turn will in like manner enlarge. Now it is not possible there can be kept up for a long series of years the requisite progression. There must be occasional deadlocks, and consequent distress; and at some point a final stop.

How different the case of farming! If the farmer is prosperous, he begins to cultivate better than he did, and so produces more food; but he treads not injuriously on his neighbour's domain. He is not much wont, or much tempted, to venture on ambitious extensions. If his success encourage an additional number of persons to engage in the business, they must either set about reclaiming waste land at home, or go abroad, where, while producing more, they are at the same time, by the employment of more labour and the uprearal of industrious families of their own, raising up consumers for their crops. This further, at any rate, is palpable: there are, with tillers of the ground and producers of animal food and wool, no sudden and overwhelming crises and times of disaster, such as shut up mills, and silence forges, and compel thousands of industrious hands to pine in idleness on the streets.

Has the nation cause to boast of the choice it has made in time past? What will be the verdict of posterity? What is the permanent product of our ascendancy in manufactures and commerce, of its alluring splendour and its refined luxuriousness? During the last half-century British statesmen had two grand openings for the profitable occupation, within the realm, of our increasing population and capital—employment in manufactures, shipping, and mines, and employment in agriculture and fisheries. They have persistently preferred the former, to the neglect, in a very great measure, of the latter—the stabler and the better of the two. If they had shown the same ardour to find outlets for the yearly increase of our people in this last direction, as they have in the former, farms at home might possibly not have been competed for so keenly, or taken on terms so inconsistent with the interests of tenants; and wages for labour on the land might have been dearer; but the Colonies would ere now have surpassed the Mother Country in population, and that population, transferred and rapidly multiplied, would be wealthy, far, far beyond their actual experience or most flattering dreams; while she would contain within her borders far fewer paupers, far fewer of the dangerous classes and the down-draughts, who are our reproach and our loss, and who, if we allow the more worthy portion to hive off, leaving the infirm and the dregs, may be our ruin.

It is time, high time, for our rulers, for the people, to awake. Tell us why we should not devise and do now, at length, what it would have been wise and well we had been doing all through the last half-century. Why not bestow on agriculture, especially in the Colonies, at least as much attention and thought as the generation before us bestowed on manufactures and trade? Extension of employment so obtained will not be chequered and checked by disastrous strikes and locks-out. It will be less fluctuating and more remunerative than that in gigantic manufactories; its supplanting which would make us infinitely more independent, for then we need not fetter ourselves with embarrassing treaties. We would be able to arrange our fiscal systems, and pursue our diplomacy, without unmanly granting or mean cringing for commercial and other favours. We would not practise nor require, for trade sake as is falsely supposed, to defend the queer neutrality which supplies one of two belligerents with coals for his fleet and Chassepôts for his armed citizens. The millions would be more contented, because more thriving, more healthy, and more happy. The relations between the home and the outlying portions of the Empire would be brought into harmony more complete and sweet.

Never has there been a grander area for the reciprocation of the good offices which supply and demand play in the Divine economy of the world. What the Colonists want is men to cultivate their virgin soil. These we can give. What the old country wants is land. That we have enabled the Colonies to give. What a host of healthy, sturdy, loyal subjects might our good Queen soon so have! If, unfortunately, the next thirty years shall be unmarked by any definite policy in this hopeful direction, what will become the position of our country? Her millions, sunk beneath burdens of taxation rendered all the more oppressive because the busiest and the best of her sons have bid her adieu for ever, will find themselves yearly less and less able to maintain their struggle with foreigners, who will yearly more and more obtrude themselves into the very shopkeeping and minor trades even of our own cities, towns, and villages. Our national development will be stunted. The slow train must be shunted. We shall be left far behind by other Empires. Even unfortunate France, especially if she fortify her position by alliances—notably Germany, Russia, and the United States—are already more populous—shall I say more powerful?—than the United Kingdom and the Colonies, all told. The three last-named Powers are expanding and increasing still.

We have the same advantages, perhaps greater than they. Do we mean to utilize these? Is it not more than possible that we are casting them away? What if our demeanour towards the Colonies—such a paltry economy, for instance, as our ceasing to fire the gun that marks a fortress as British—should lead to estrangement, and estrangement to declarations of Independence? We have sometimes—aye, too often—spoken and acted in a way calculated to estrange. No doubt we have been liberal in our concessions in things substantial. This very liberality has its dark side. We have gone so far, that we must go farther. What we have done is not enough. A satisfactory answer must be given to the question, What benefit do the Colonies receive now, or have they to expect, from their connexion with us and with one another? We allow them no preference in our markets. If they were foreigners, they would have the same advantages. Deprived of their early privileges, they now obtain little more from us than the British ægis in case of war. Moreover, this advantage is equivocal; for, say some, they are more likely to be involved in war through us.

I rejoice that we, even in peace, have still great favours

to bestow. We can establish a national and patriotic system of Emigration to the Colonies. We can, under the auspices of the august Head of the State, inaugurate a new Imperial policy, which will tend to diffuse throughout the Empire the capital, and "well-to-do" persons from the nobleman to the peasant and the artizan, which superabound or "congest" at the Empire's heart. Thereby new life and a fresh spring of energy would everywhere burst forth.

Highly as I rate these favours, wholesome and heartsome as I am sure their influence would be, they are in my sight as nothing, for the end in view, compared with the cherishing of a national spirit. May we not learn much in this respect from our neighbours? What a practical love of *la belle France*, what pride in it and sticking to it, has the volatile Frenchman! How has devotion for the Fatherland stirred up and knit together in self-sacrifice the phlegmatic German! Who has such conspicuous tall talk, and, as its basis, elevated, efficacious conceptions regarding "our country," as the citizen of the United States? Call forth, then, a stronger national sentiment.

Realize simultaneously the possibilities of our future. What a grand ground-work has been laid by our fathers! Are we sure we do not degenerate? With the good old toast, "Ships, Colonies, and Commerce," have disappeared other evidences of the ancient *amor patriæ*. What, at any rate, to descend to humbler particulars, is the reception Colonists experience when they come "home" for life, or on visits? Who gives them welcome? and of what kind is it? There is no "*houff*," no home-warmth, at the Colonial Office, nor anywhere in London. If the administration of that part of the Empire were conducted by a Board composed of leading men who have dwelt for a time in some Colony, or otherwise are recognized as authorities on Colonial questions, and if the Colonial Office thereby became, as it might and should be, the frequent, pleasant, and natural house of call, the case would be different quite. Royalty and nobility might then recognize a now unfelt personal duty, and now unseen splendid opportunities to serve the State.

Without in any way imputing deficiencies in time past, the future points, in the interest of the Throne and the Peerage both of which we wish to maintain in efficiency for the sake of the Constitutional liberties and order that form their *raison d'être*, to a more palpable, active, and loyal discharge of the pertinent functions, as hereafter essential to their successful operation. The Queen, when in that health which we much wish to see restored, ought to be accessible to Colonists, not for consultation, but as the social head and leader of the nation. The *entrée* into Buckingham Palace might make them feel they are "at home," when appreciatedly welcomed by the highest and the legitimate exponent of the nation's mind and affections.

As to the Nobles, who will follow suit, remember how in old times they were expected to be at the call of the Sovereign. They had to fight for their country, and that beyond seas. In later days we have instances of better leadership during peace, in the first occupation of transatlantic lands. But what thus rarely has been done by individuals ought to be the work and glory of the class. The laws ought to be changed so as to permit subdivision of large estates among sons, without regard to primogeniture, wherever the estate is large enough to suffer partition without its derogating from the sufficiency of the eldest son's means to uphold the rank assigned him and to perform its requirements. Especially there should be facility and encouragement given everybody to exchange lands in the British counties for larger tracts in the Colonies.

The greater the sacrifice made for country's sake, the more honour is due. The more remote the position chosen, and the more arduous and expensive the reclaiming work, the more recognition should be made of service so rendered to the Empire. Stars of India and Orders of St. Michael and St. George—or, recalling the past, Knighthoods of Nova Scotia—are valuable as a partial acknowledgment by Royalty that the Empire is one; but they fall short in this respect, that they mark a distinction between its parts. They are not Imperial, and they are even *extra* British.

What the emergency demands is bold, hearty, unmistakeable, practical avowal by our rulers and by Parliament, that the people at home and the people in the Colonies are alike and equally fellow-subjects, and are to be dealt with as fellow-workers in the common cause, indiscriminate participators of the ancestral honours and hereditary privileges of the nation, as well as permanently responsible, as joint guardians, for their transmission to future generations.

The United Kingdom has been called " Mother

of Nations." I dislike the expression. It too well consists with that separation of interests and severance from the Throne which we reprobate and deprecate. But I have no objection to any modification of it that may imply that, while the Mother Country is a home for all the children, the people who still inhabit the British Isles claim no superiority nor even precedence, except what depends on their being more numerous, over the other *States* or Provinces which form the Empire.

Let us, if you will, regard the old country as a "Mother of States;" of States as free and independent as the United Kingdom, rendering allegiance as hearty and as abiding to the same Sovereign, who is loyal, like them, to the *Constitution* in which we rejoice.

At a recent conference in Liverpool a speaker compared the relationship between the British Isles and the Colonies to that between parents and children, and, resting on his similitude, drew the unpleasant inference that a time must come when the parental house should be left and the filial tie be broken. Surely the connexion resembles rather that between a number of sons or brothers associated in a commercial firm. You know that there are no partnerships so harmonious, so successful, and so lasting, as those constituted in this manner. Perhaps the similitude may be carried a step further. The original " firm " may be supposed to have founded in various parts of the world thriving branch establishments, managed by partners who are members of the family. These establishments have been supplied with large capital, and trusted with great responsibilities, for the general behoof. The capital I refer to is, in the actual circumstances, lands acquired by our fathers. Their liability to hold these for the family or firm ought to form an insuperable barrier to separation. No one branch can disconnect itself without the consent of every other. The property and profit of each belongs to all.

Leaving metaphor, let us address ourselves to the facts of the case in hand. The Parliament of the United Kingdom has begun to act as if the several "countries" which compose the British Empire (not reckoning among these India, which is altogether an exceptional dependency) are sister or brother States, and that the Colonies have outgrown the distinctive character which belongs to daughters or sons. All these countries, no doubt, so far as their internal or municipal affairs are concerned, enjoy, or may look forward to, self-government and independent action; but there is, up to the present moment, no practical exercise or recognition of their right or title to share in the regulation of Imperial affairs, in the government of the Empire.

It is unreasonable to stop short without this crowning concession. The Colonists have an equal interest in the Empire's good government, are equally liable to suffer from its bad government, and are as competent to judge what should be the nation's policy and to express the nation's wish and will. How can we expect that Colonists, intelligent and prosperous, accustomed to Parliamentary debates and to the business of governing, will submit longer to the exclusion to which our want of prevision still subjects them?

Who of us can allege that the wisdom of the British Parliament and Government is so indisputable, and their knowledge of the extremities of the Empire so intuitive, that the addition of these counsels and the infusion of new vigour would not tend to a better system of rule? Whether or no, besides, the amount of work which all departments of Government and both Houses of Parliament have to face and scamper through (or scamp) is such, that it has practically come to this: the considering of Colonial questions and advising with the Colonies has almost fallen into complete abeyance. During the last few sessions of Parliament, how very little time has been bestowed even on the important subjects of this paper! How difficult has it been to find time for them! How have they, when actually brought forward, been slurred over!

What sympathy has been shown Colonists at the Colonial Office? How much leisure has the Colonial Minister been able to give for free and easy conning over and communing on Colonial affairs? Is there any rational ground to hope for a healthier state of things in the future? None.

The experience and the anticipation of Colonists, even with regard to matters that come under their cognizance, cannot satisfy them that exclusion from all voice in the determination of questions that affect the Empire, is innocuous, and continuance of the *status quo* reasonable and defensible. Not less must they see and feel that to send representatives to sit in the British Parliament would in no promising degree make matters better. Such representatives would deem it impertinent to vote on questions affecting only the British Islands. Motions carried by a majority dependent on Colonial votes would be resented among ourselves. The increased length and number of discussions on Colonial questions would only still more overburden Parliament; and, after all, the Colonists could hardly expect to exert their legitimate influence and power either on Colonial or Imperial measures. Objections of the same character and weight cannot be alleged to a proposition which has often been made, with differences in details, to representatives of the principal Colonies sitting at a *Colonial Board,* such as I have already spoken of, presided over by the Colonial Minister; but, then, such a representatives would not touch the question presently before us, and would not mitigate the evils, or meet the claims, we are presently discussing.

If the proposition were to admit representatives of the principal Colonies to places in the *Cabinet,* the only objection that could be raised is the incongruity of burdening them with the responsibility of deciding questions which do not affect the Colonies nor the Empire, but the British Islands only. I apprehend we are shut up to one conclusion and one course. That course perfectly satisfies some. If others can show a better, let them. Till then, and in its absence, we may be allowed to maintain and urge that the most or the only logical procedure is to superimpose over the several Parliaments and Administrations of the United Kingdom and the Colonies an *Imperial representative Cabinet or Council,* invested, under the Queen, with supreme power to act as a Legislature and Executive for the Empire. To such a body would be entrusted the determination of questions of peace or war, of contributions of men and money for naval and military purposes, of international treaties, and of all laws affecting the Empire as a whole.

I do not conceive that there is any objection on principle to a Council invested with these great powers. It would work much more easily than it could have done but a few years ago, seeing Colonial representatives can now with lightning speed communicate with their several "countries."

The Colonies would probably hail the establishment of such a Council as a complimentary concession, as well as a positive advantage. They could not but feel just pride in being called on to take part in the great Council of the Empire.

The inhabitants of the old country might not so easily reconcile themselves to their amended relationship. Some might represent it as a "coming down in the world." Others might apprehend that the new machinery would not work smoothly. To these and every hesitant an appeal must be made in the plainest terms, and in the most earnest language : Are you, or are you not, prepared for the alternative—disruption of the Empire, the severance from the Mother Country of the more important Colonies?

Let us not blink matters. There has been a portentous change. If we do not direct it aright, it will culminate in revolution. Negligence on the part of the British Parliament, and *insouciance* on that of British

Governments, during the last quarter of a century, have allowed a few individuals or theorists to speak *ex cathedra*, and even to act with authority of office, in such a manner as to cause loyal Colonists to believe, and a few to allege openly, that the connexion of the Colonists with the Mother Country is regarded at home as a burden, and that their value to her is so disparaged, and the reciprocal claims, to which I at least attach the greatest importance, so attenuated, that we would willingly " let friends part as friends."

I need not multiply quotations from public documents and the public press, to establish this appalling charge. Unfortunately, inculpatory proofs are as plentiful as blackberries at this season. I merely quote a short extract from private letters which I have received within the last two or three months.

A relation of my own writes in August from Canada : " The Liberal party, whose policy evidently is to throw Canada into the arms of the United States. . . . It is a great pity, as the bulk of the Canadian populalation are loyal to the heart's core, and justly proud of their connexion with Great Britain. We had an instance lately. The Independence-Annexation-Fenian party brought up a candidate " [in my correspondent's own district] " to oppose the nominee of the loyal party," &c. . . . " The gentlemen of the Irish persuasion invariably supported the Annexation candidate. . . . Many of us are deeply grieved to see the Imperial Government abandoning the time-honoured and historic fortresses of Quebec and Kingston. It looks like leaving us to our fate."

Looks beguile. I am ready to distrust them here. It is to the credit of the present Government that they have avowed a settled purpose to assist the Colonies in case of war. How can they fulfil the promise and engagement on the present system, and without more concert with the Colonies? This *en passant*.

Another friend, a member of one of the Australian Legislatures, writes me: "At a Congress at Melbourne, for the purpose of a Customs Union, ideas are rather going in the direction of Independence altogether and confederation of the various Colonies."

Observe the use of the word *Independence* in both letters. Plainly, we are reaping as we have sown. If there is not disaffection, certainly indifference has been engendered. Happily, there is no ground for disaffection; happily, whatever indifference does exist admits of being removed, and that by moving on in the very direction indicated in the second of these communications—that is, by conceding independence, conceding it in the sense and way of confederation; in other words, enlarging the Imperial Constitution in such manner as to admit of the Colonies being put on a par with the United Kingdom in the government of the Empire. In case any one should conceive that separation of the Colonies can be effected without injury to the Mother Country, I ask him again to look to other nations. See France, occupied by a population much more numerous than that of the British Isles; yet it is supposed that even she, in order to greater magnitude, will seek to bring into alliance and unity of action with herself the contiguous peninsulas. See Germany, formerly composed of separate parts bound clumsily together, crystallizing into one mass. See Russia, with a vast population, drawing to herself, with bearlike hugging, adjoining States. See the United States, with a population as great as that of Great Britain and the Colonies superadded. These last continue still to increase or grow, to grow rapidly. Knowing that a nation's strength and independence is in proportion to the number of fighting men and consequently of its people, taken in connexion with the compactness and defensibleness of its soil, and observing that the war spirit is not dead nor dying in the world, need one ask: Is this a time to be indifferent as to the magnitude of the population of the British Empire, and be careless whether we, as a nation, grow stronger or weaker?

India we cannot take into account. The hundred and fifty or eighty millions there may be weakness as much as strength. If strength, this arises, in no small degree, from the strength of the rest of the Empire. Part with the Colonies, and we weaken our hold of India. We prepare the way for troubles, and invite movements and agitations that might eventuate in loss of our dominion there, and of the *prestige* and power which possessing it gives.

The isolated position of the several parts of our Empire is also, in one point of view, weakness, but in another, strength. It exposes us at a great many points to attack. It is difficult, or impossible, to defend so extended frontiers, and so long and so many coast-lines.

On the other hand, the loss of a part does not endanger other parts. The *whole* of our territories cannot be overrun by an enemy, and we derive the benefit of places of security, replenishment, and repair for our navy and military at a great multiplicity of what, in varied circumstances, may prove to be positions of importance. After all, however, these are secondary considerations. A great and strong Power is normally and usually at peace with other nations. The possession of harbours and depôts is then of unequivocal and unmixed advantage. It is our own fault if we do not turn them to very profitable account.

" Oh," says he who is free-trader and nothing else, " under the beautiful and benign cosmopolitanism which Cobden preached and Britain practises, all nations and all flags are destined to have equal advantages. Let the Colonies be abandoned, and even fall into the arms of foreign Powers, our trade would be unaffected. They'd still welcome our ships, and receive our cargoes, and send us their wealth." Friend, who are content with so little, can you be sure even of this? Will slighted love and spurned advances not breed coldness, or aversion, or retaliation? Will the protectionism which shelters and disguises itself as virtue, under the plea that blood is thicker than water, and charity begins at home, not overthrow existing commercial arrangements, and intensify tariffs that are adverse enough now, so as to be positively subversive of commerce? However, no complaints! We are deeply thankful for the extent of profitable business that we actually do with the

Colonies. Let me illustrate, by means of a few figures kindly furnished me by the ex-President of the Liverpool Chamber of Commerce. These show how much more largely than foreigners, man for man, Colonists trade with us :—

COMPARATIVE IMPORT AND EXPORT PER HEAD OF THE POPULATION TO THE FOLLOWING FOREIGN COUNTRIES*—VIZ. :—

	Population.	Exports. and Imports.	Rate per head. £ s. d.
Russia	74,000,000	£27,250,000	0 7 4
France	38,000,000	57,410,000	1 10 0
Italy	24,000,000	9,250,000	0 7 6
Austria	34,670,000	3,270,000	0 1 8
Turkey in Europe	15,500,000	12,700,000	0 16 0
Holland	3,756,000	28,000,000	7 10 0
Belgium	5,000,000	16,600,000	3 2 0
United States	34,500,000	66,800,000	1 18 0
Brazil	10,000,000	12,940,000	1 5 0
	239,426,000	£234,220,000	Less than 20s. per head.

To the following British Possessions :—

North America	4,250,000	12,000,000	2 17 6
West Indies	1,000,000	9,500,000	9 10 0
Australia	1,500,000	25,500,000	16 0 0
Singapore	300,000	3,600,000	12 0 0
Cape	260,000	4,300,000	18 0 0
	7,310,000	£54,900,000; or £7 10s. per head.	

* The trade with India is at the rate of only about 7s. per head, but that country is not a "Colony." The framer of the table wishes it understood that it is not intended to be minutely accurate.

There is one inestimable advantage which the British Empire enjoys in common with three of the great Powers of the world. This advantage is presented to us only in and through the Colonies. I mean the possession of large unoccupied territories. France has something of the kind, but only in Algeria, and there under conditions which neutralize its benefits—a burning climate and hostile rightful claimants. Russia is so sparsely populated that her vast area is not needed in order to sustain an increasing population. The United States are in circumstances exactly like ours. They have vast tracts still open, and in a temperate climate. Probably, immigrants from Great Britain would reach the extreme far West, even California, more cheaply than South Africa or Australasia. But on the debtor side of the account must be placed distance from the sea; and the lanky look of the American may well occasion doubt whether Europeans will thrive, even in body, over there as well as in the British Possessions.

The philosophy and good sense of the case is, let Britons be content and grateful, and keep together. Nationally, we can hardly, if at all, be situated better than we are. If our superior advantages are not seen by some men, remove the film from these short-sighted eyes. If quite well seen, and yet perilously slighted, the more shame. But there is no great good in self-reproach. Enough that we reverse erroneous procedure. The earlier we make known our determination to hold the Colonies firmly, the better. There is no second unoccupied world for us to conquer and colonize.

Great Britain and the United States (inheritrix on a title we don't care to dispute) own and possess all the fertile and accessible tracts of the globe.

Observance of British antecedents, and consciousness of the nobleness of British policy, warrant us to believe, what other nations will not hesitate to admit, that the retirement of Great Britain from her place of pre-eminence and its opportunities, her relinquishment of the post which Providence and mankind assign her, would be a just and great and perpetual subject of world-wide lamentation. Why should we retire voluntarily and unnecessarily? We may hope, if not attacked too suddenly and by combined force, and if repressing impracticable meddlesomeness, to stand our ground.

How much stronger will the Empire be by-and-by, when, through judicious encouragement of emigration and presentment of facilities for the cultivation of waste lands, the Colonies shall have doubled the Empire's population and strength! Friendship, or alliance, with such a Power as we shall then be, will and must be sought and valued. If the Anglo-Saxon, or rather—for we forget not the Celts—the English-speaking races, act in harmony, with no jealousies among themselves, they will form a coalition which no nation dare oppose, yet none need fear; for its power will never be exercised adversely to mankind. For this reason, if for no other, let the United States and our "United Empire" act and feel towards each other as if the day may not be distant, and ought, by interchange of kind offices and reciprocation of courteous respect, to be accelerated, when both will be cemented in the warmest, as it will be the most natural and congenial, of alliances.

Why may I not express, what I rejoice to discover is a cherished thought in many earnest and large hearts—hope, rising almost to anticipation, that the United States of South America and "the United States of the Britannic Empire" will, a century hence, be federated together, as not merely geographically, but morally, a great "Atlantica" and "Pacifica,"— *Atlantic*, as being the realization of the fabled sustainer of the world in its place and order, by means of quiet, concentrated strength; and *Pacific*, as the keeper of the world's peace, by its diffused healthful influence.

With the Germans, now in the ascendant, all these federable States have the ties of blood-relationship and love of religious freedom and simplicity. With the French, the Celtic element in Scotland, Ireland, and Canada makes us akin. With the Russians, we will be close neighbours in the East and in the North, without adequate motive for jealousies and unworthy rivalries.

Is this picture painted in too glowing colours? Is there no dark back-ground? There may possibly be a hidden wish, in quarters where our type of civilization, and liberty, and religion is feared and distrusted, that the United Kingdom should decline in influence. Some, with this in view, may insidiously favour disintegration. *Cavete canes.* Undoubtedly I have indulged my imagination by conceiving a bright future.

It is with the present we have to do. Our immediate concern is to counteract any disintegrative tendency, and to prevent its development. There is no wisdom in letting the ships of a fleet drift apart. Our Admiral should give forth the word that will keep us together, and lead us on the right course. His trumpet must not give forth a faint nor an uncertain sound. Why should our statesmen, like the parent who was "very old," and "heard all that his sons did" without restraining, feebly say with him, "Why do ye such things? for I hear of your evil dealings by all this people. Nay, my sons, for it is no good report that I hear." I wish that some of the most prominent went even thus far. They even speak of "educating" our Colonists for such a catastrophe, as if it were a merit to lead on thereto! It is high time to wake up and wage war against such disturbers. Let us beware especially of undermining operations, and cease to confer honours on men who openly advocate secession.

To be practical: let the British family be summoned together for a family council. The Colonists will there tell all that is in their mind. We shall learn what they wish. They will be able not only to speak for themselves, and disarm our minds of fears which sheer ignorance and distance (not always lending enchantment to a view) may have generated and fostered. They will add wisdom, vigour, and impulse to our deliberations and our acts. All have a common and imperial cause in hand; let there be a common and imperial character given to these deliberations and acts.

The case is undoubtedly urgent. Every mail brings fresh evidence and tidings of mischief brewing. If there are to be consultations and negotiations (and where several parties are to enter into an agreement negotiations there must be), a time of harmony is always the most opportune. Such a time is the present. There is nowhere any jarring just now. The period, therefore, is eminently favourable; and a good excuse, a ready occasion, a sufficient motive, is at this very moment happily presented. The United Kingdom is moved on the subject of its national defences and armaments, which are admittedly inadequate for the contingency of sudden emergencies. The same negligence, or false security, in virtue of which we have inconsiderately been slumbering at home, has prevailed in the Colonies. Yet there it is as necessary as here that there should be devised beforehand, and prepared for the demands of required instant service, a thorough system of naval and military armaments. But who shall prescribe their mode and extent, and command actual performance of the work? The Colonial Minister cannot do this of himself. The Cabinet cannot. Parliament would shrink from the responsibility as too venturesome, even if it possessed the necessary qualification and aptitude.

The object cannot be attained in any serviceable time and manner by correspondence. The business is too complicated for that. It does not brook slowness and delays. The condition is unexampled. The right to determine and execute practically lies with others, who, if they do not require to be conciliated, at least (and that not merely from courtesy, but in the very nature of the case) need to be consulted and worked with heartily as any principal co-operators. Would that the Government saw and felt all this. Surely a "*pro re nata* council of the Empire," however informally, and in spite of there being no precedents for such a course, ought to be immediately convened. Their deliberations would, as a matter of course, but by no means as a matter for regret, diverge and expand, so as to comprehend other cognate subjects on which it is desirable and important that all parts of the Empire should arrive at a common understanding. There are many points connected with our legislation that demand attention. There are many questions on which our remoter fellow-subjects are entitled and able to make weighty representations. One of their propositions will, probably, be a supreme and permanent Council for the Empire—such as that which it is the chief object of this paper to recommend and promote. I hope it will be so. I have little anxiety as to the course of events.

To sum up my convictions and aspirations, may I again revert to early history for apposite words? To an ancient mother it was said, as Providence is now saying to the Mother Country, "I will multiply thy seed exceedingly, that it shall not be numbered for multitude." "Arise! lift up the lad, and hold him in thine hand, for I will make him a great nation." In the same venerable record we find addressed to another mother a filial remonstrance, which I give the Colonies the credit of adopting: "Entreat me not to leave thee, or to return from following after thee; for whither thou goest, I will go, and where thou lodgest, I will lodge. Thy people shall be my people, and thy God my God. Where thou diest I will die, and there will I be buried. The Lord do so to me, and more also, if aught but death part thee and me."

THE UNITED KINGDOM AND COLONIES ONE AUTONOMIC EMPIRE.

A PAPER READ BEFORE THE ASSOCIATION FOR THE PROMOTION OF SOCIAL SCIENCE, AT BRISTOL, 1869.

That regard for liberty and equity which characterizes the law and rule and diplomatic action of our country, warrant our belief that the permanence of her place and influence, as a first-class Power, is a matter to be desired for the sake of the great world among whose nations she has so wonderfully acquired a commanding position.

A people may be powerful by reason either of moral influence or of natural strength. Practically, the former, which is the nobler and more valuable attainment, cannot subsist effectually if not associated with the latter, the coarser and more common-place attribute. This strength is relative. A nation may become weaker even while its resources are as great, and its people as many and as brave as ever, if other nations are outstripping it in resources and particularly in numbers, either by the natural growth of population, or by emigration, or by extension of populated territory. Russia, Germany, and the United States, are at this moment much ahead of the United Kingdom in the number of fighting men they can train for defence and attack. These Powers are also remarkably compact in respect to their territories, whereas the British Empire lies scattered in separate portions over the globe.

This diffusion is not without advantages; whether

on the whole for better or worse, it is our situation, and we accept it. This our situation involves duties. In accepting it, we assume heavy responsibilities. These duties and responsibilities, I much fear, have been generally overlooked, or, at least, are seldom boldly faced. We do not realize the grandeur of the heritage and trust which have been committed to the last and the present generation of Britons and, if the term will be allowed, Anglo-Celts. Our immediate predecessors, and we ourselves, have sought present ease and prosperity without considering earnestly what is best for the estate we are called to occupy as life-tenants and administer as trustees. I fear we have been deluding ourselves by the transparent fallacy that what contributes most to the enjoyment and wealth of the living will best serve the unborn. Is it beyond the truth of facts to suggest that we have hoodwinked ourselves into presumptuous and foolish confidence that in future there will be no costly wars, or, if there shall be such wars, that the unpaid enormous debts incurred in former wars (which were carried on far more cheaply than can be the case hereafter) will form no serious obstacle to success in them; that is, that more hundreds of millions will, notwithstanding these liabilities, be borrowed on favourable terms, and the augmented charge of interest for the doubled or trebled debt will, when peace is restored, occasion, and be, no hindrance to the nation's continued prosperity? This is the charitable construction of our acts. Unfortunately, the frivolous way in which the question, " What has posterity done for us?" is frequently put and received, conveys to thoughtful minds painful misgivings and forebodings of a less flattering character.

A principal feature of British policy since the peace of 1815 has been to stimulate manufactures and trade. Equal heed has not been given to the advantages of promoting agriculture, though this is a source of wealth which is far steadier and more unfailing than foreign trade, and an occupation that produces men of greater physical vigour than manufactures—men also better rooted and more deeply interested in the land we live in and in its Colonies. Attention to home agriculture has been left to the landlords, who, it must be said, have wonderfully developed the capabilities of the soil (except in so far as the influence of game laws and the desire of sport have restrained the tendency to reclaim). As to farming in the Colonies, considerable efforts have no doubt been put forth by the State as proprietor of waste lands, but not in a manner worthy of being regarded and praised as national policy. Without disparaging the beneficial tendency, in several points of view, of the remarkable progress of mining, manufactures, and commerce, to which we have attained, there is room to question whether our national greatness, our national stability, our national independence, our national solidarity, as well as our national present happiness and future prospects, would not have been much more thorough and satisfactory if Government and people had sought earnestly and with less distraction that the outflow of our population and the obtaining of employment had been towards agriculture at home and in British Colonial territories. Hitherto emigration, which in itself surely is a matter for anything but congratulation if we consider its causes, has not been regulated, or directed, to the extent to which it might have been, on the principle that it is better to retain the emigrant as a British subject than to have him numbered among foreigners. In the one case he would, in time of peace, be a consumer almost exclusively of British goods, and a contributor to British wealth; and, in time of war, a prized addition to the prowess and patriotism we might evoke. In the other case he would consume foreign commodities, or else British commodities heavily taxed by (his own) unsympathetic legislation, and might even be called to take up arms against his native country.

It is not too late to mend. Opportunities indeed have been missed, millions of our best sons and daughters are now citizens of the United States; but we have few wrongs to redress, little or no legislation to undo. If we have erred, it has been in the spirit of a free nation. Our people have been left free to go wherever they liked. Our Colonies have been allowed to frame their own laws, and impose whatever duties they thought fit, I shall not say even to the unnatural extent of commercial parricide, but, speaking euphemistically, of commercial suicide. They are loyal to our beloved Sovereign and to the Constitution. They cannot but appreciate the treatment they have received. If our relationship had been as it was of old, when their trade was restricted by exclusive regard to the interests of the Mother Country (I prefer to use that word which comes, and ever will come, to our ears and hearts with more dearness and tenderness than does "Fatherland" to the Germans), we would not at this day have been addressing them through British governors with the excessive frankness which has just awakened our fellow-subjects to a sense of their new position of recognized equality and of liberty to judge and act no longer as our children, but as full-grown though younger brothers and adult members of the British family. Their rulers are in little danger of supposing that what is really complimentary, and a recognition of the rights and powers they have achieved, is an expression of British indifference to the connexion that subsists between us. On the contrary, we would feel pain to part; but we are averse to claim the right and power which theoretically belongs to us to overrule their decisions and shape their destinies. We hail them now, not as Dependencies, but as parts of the same Empire, participants of our ancient and noble privileges, and sharers of our grand responsibilities. Both they and we see that in union is our strength. The bundle of rods must and will be kept together. Like the patriarch, we all say, and the Colonies most especially, "With a staff we crossed the waters, and now we are become bands, strong and many, bound together as one." When other States of the world are growing in number of subjects and extent of territory, it would be a matter for unbounded regret if the British Empire were to shiver into fragments. Therefore we will not part from one another, if it is possible, as we know it is, to maintain the union that has been so long enjoyed. Let us rather consult together how best to consolidate and weld or fuse into one mass what is in nature congenial, and is already warm. Even now the comprehending of the Colonies in the census of British subjects, without including in the aggregate the vast population of India, shows that, in point of peopled territory, we are entitled to a proud, but I trust not abused, pre-eminence among the nations? To how much more, when we take into account the tendency of Anglo-Saxons and Anglo-Celts to multiply and replenish, in a few years may we expect to grow? I see no reason why we should not be able in half-a-century to count equal to the greatest Powers then sharing the beneficent domination of this earth.

We at home require, however, to recall the Colonies to greater consciousness of the fact, and the value to themselves, of their British origin and connexion. We and they require to reconstitute our reciprocal relationship, if not on a firmer, at least on a new basis. As for us, we must not merely appeal to our claims on them and their claims on us, but show ourselves worthy of their admiration and confidence. We must so act as to make them court amalgamation. A feeling of this kind cannot be relied upon if our British policy continues so selfish and so short-sighted as it has been. We must no longer rest satisfied with ourselves, while making no attempt, even the feeblest, at once to reduce and finally to remove our prodigious and disgraceful debt of eight hundred millions. What are our honest fellow-subjects—not to say the open-eyed citizens of other States—to conclude, when a popular Chancellor of the Exchequer, in answer to a recent motion in the House of Commons calling attention to this subject, points with more than complacency to the fact that for the last few years three millions and odd sterling per annum have, casually and certainly without set purpose, been written off by the favourable circumstance of there being surplus revenue.* They cannot but contrast the stout and successful efforts, made at no small personal cost, of the people of the United States to extinguish, as is expected to be done within fifteen, or at the utmost twenty-five years, the heavy debt which imposes on those States the payment of interest not much short of our own annual burden. Seeing we are utterly indisposed to do our duties in peace, how can we expect that the Colonists will maintain, if they can escape it, relationship with a Power that, so far from preparing itself in peace for the fresh debts which war is too sure to bring, is actually making itself effeminate, by avoiding, with equivocal morality or unequivocal immorality, that necessary hardship of bearing taxes and denying ourselves luxuries, which would form a valuable training for evil times that may come, God only knows how soon. It is much the same with regard to our armaments, naval and military. How can we hope that Colonies will esteem a people which—in these times, when other

---

* During last Session the House of Commons, with approval of the right honourable gentleman, passed unanimously a motion in favour of gradually reducing the National Debt.

Powers are armed and ready for the conflict, and although its territories are so much more exposed by extent of shore-line and wide distribution—unabashed acknowledges that time is required for the raising, equipping, and training of a sufficiency of soldiers, and the building and manning of a sufficiency of ships of war for her safety ; in other and plain words, that she, as a rule, keeps herself unready ?

Doing what becomes us, what indeed is incumbent on us, as at once a first-class Power and a Mother Country, we may confidently look for alliance, or confederation, or unification ; and we need not fear that, if we on our side admit or allow the claim of thriving Colonies to equality, regulated by due regard to numbers, they will be backward in recognizing equity as the basis on which the regenerated Empire shall be governed in the matter of State burdens and State services. In so far as debt has been, and expenses shall hereafter be, incurred for interests common to them and to us, doubt not the Colonies will be ready to assume and bear their fair share. They will be ready to raise soldiers or pay for those we raise for national defence, in just proportion.

We have hitherto held these reasonable expectations in abeyance. Colonial matters have hitherto occupied a very small place in the minds either of our statesmen or our Parliaments. In consequence of this, there has not only been remissness in the important matters just adverted to, but slackness, which I for one characterize as culpable, with regard to maintenance of British proprietary rights in British territories.

Ask leading, perhaps even official statesmen, to whom belong unoccupied lands, acquired by the bravery of our troops or our seamen, and the enterprise of our navigators and pioneers, and you will be surprised how hazy, if not how erroneous, is the answer you will receive. But this is only in keeping with their disclaimer of liability to share the expense of defending from internal disturbances; a disclaimer untenable if Britain still owns lands, for such she would, of course, contribute to hold. We are apt to forget that the British rights in our Possessions are two-fold. As we should not relinquish or have relinquished *proprietorship* in unoccupied lands,* though we would wisely conjoin in it the Colonist as administrators for the new " State body," so we ought not to relinquish the imperial right of *superiority* over lands sold and occupied, with all that is involved; most precious is the hereditament if we are to continue one great nation.

The approaching conference,† summoned by leading

---

* At the late meetings at which Mr. Macfie rendered an account of his stewardship, he characterized the way in which the United Kingdom has, without debate in Parliament, and without receiving any equivalent or even stipulating for any share of or control over the proceeds of sales, divested herself of the whole lands and territories she possessed till within the last few years in our thriving Colonies, as " playing ducks and drakes " with these costly and valuable national properties, right to deal with which at the present time might have presented a ready and useful means of relief from difficulties connected with Ireland, and with the depression of trade in Great Britain.— *Note*, 1869.

† The suggested Conference was discouraged by the British Government, and not favoured in the Colonies, and never met.

Colonists, we who are here rejoice in. We approve of the order of Knighthood by which the Queen has shown the Colonies that they are still "of us, though not locally with us." Visits of Royal Princes point in the same good direction. But very much more must be aimed at. I trust, difficult as the work is, good progress towards mastering it will be made by the present congress as well as by the conference that is summoned.

The Lords have, in relation to the Colonial part of this Empire, great functions and great opportunities. The Upper House may well make this subject a speciality. Their Lordships may reckon on the support of the House of Commons in any practical propositions which it may please them to make for facilitating, even on the principle of sub-division in favour of younger sons, the exchange of valuable estates in the British Isles for large unoccupied districts over the seas. There I have no doubt, without any diminution of *prestige* and power at home, but rather with vast increase of these, the great abilities and manly virtues, and other high qualities which so honourably distinguish our aristocracy, would be seduced and exercised far more than at home in the comparative inactivity which is here their doom. Who can estimate how much this "birzing yont" (to adopt the homely phrase, with the tactics, of a Scottish noble of the olden time) would promote not only their own happiness, but the strengthening of the Colonial connexion with Britain, the expansion of the Empire, and the welfare of mankind? Then our dukes will show themselves truly *duces;* our marquises will really, conforming to their name, occupy and defend the place of honour and trust at the marches and outposts; and earls and barons will no longer bear titles of dignity apart from the State services these formerly implied that they were ready to render.

The presence of a standing Council, composed of the weightiest and most sagacious of our fellow-subjects, congregated from every quarter of the globe—which advantage a better connexion with the Colonies would insure—would introduce even into our domestic legislation new and masculine vigour, and would enable us to command that respect which is so advantageous, with a view to the preservation of peace within the deservedly fostered British dominions in the East, and to the avoidance of dangerous pretensions from foreign Governments.

A word in conclusion, which I hope will not bring on me the smiles of *bathos*-haters. Let us cease to use the word " Imperial " to designate what belongs merely to this kingdom, and give it full and appropriate significance as denoting what belongs to the " Empire " of which this kingdom, however much it shall prosper, may, we hope, become, by the growth of our Colonies, but a minor portion.

LETTER TO A PROMINENT MEMBER OF THE CABINET.

ASHFIELD HALL, NESTON,
5th September, 1870.

MY DEAR SIR,—In your obliging letter of 31st August, you well stated the aim of the policy, imperfectly understood by my Canadian correspondent, to be "strength, union, and consolidation." In my acknowledgment of the 1st inst., I readily assumed that this statesmanly object has regard not merely to the British Possessions in America, but to the whole Empire. I know from the declarations you and Lord Granville made in Parliament no longer ago than last session, that the unity and substantial integrity of the Empire it is the determination of the Government to maintain. (I have already expressed my fear that the opportunity or possibility of perfecting and securing the strength and power of the Empire by consolidation in the form of federal connexion is slipping away. Every mail that arrives from Australia and Africa furnishes additional ground for this fear. To-day I receive from Queensland a letter, dated 11th July, in which my correspondent, a most intelligent member of the Parliament of the Colony, writes:—

" As regards politics, Australia seems on the whole not inclined to have a closer connexion with the Mother Country than at present exists. The people seem quite satisfied with the privileges they possess, and I do not think they will like the idea of a consolidation with the Empire. At a congress at Melbourne (the proceedings of which are interesting to you), for the purpose of a Customs Union—the ideas are going in the direction of Independence altogether, and Confederation of the various Colonies."

The Independence my friend points at means disintegration of the Empire. Disintegration means weakness of the parts into which it would decompose. Such weakness of the United Kingdom is not mere national calamity from which there would be recovery, but an irreparable loss to the world. The people at home and, I am satisfied, the people in the Colonies—whatever a handful of theorists may have said in favour of it, or done in a direction towards it—are opposed in heart to the separation of the Mother Country from the Colonies, and of the Colonies from one another (if, indeed, they can be said to be opposed to a policy of rending, of which they have not only got no notice, but have not contemplated the possibility). I hope I may say the same is the case with the British Parliament. It is certainly so with the constituencies.

Events now hurry on so fast, and politicians have now so many surprises, that (allow me to say it, with great deference) the Government will be held justified in the eyes of all men if it takes the initiative at once in proceeding to prevent, by anticipation, agitation or action intended to dismember. Such agitation may be the insidious work of enemies who see in the power of our country and the tendencies of the time influences on behalf of liberty and of mankind which they dislike; or, and this is the probability, it will be the natural expression of dissatisfaction with a state of mutual relations which the Colonies have outgrown. I do not wonder at the dissatisfaction. It must be met by a recognition of existing facts and prospective wants. The whole Empire, and not the United Kingdom only, must be independent or self-governing.

Some connexion on the principle of equality and equity must be formed—call it a "Federation"—resembling in a good measure that by which the United States are bound together in strong happy oneness. If the alternative of such a connexion with the Mother Country and the rest of the Empire, or separation and isolation, be presented now, there can be little doubt, or no doubt at all, *which* the several Colonies will prefer. As to the United Kingdom, I am convinced it is ripe for the proposition. Even if such had not been the case before the present dreadful war, the events of the last few weeks show all men that a nation's strength depends in no small degree upon its numbers. Strip away the Colonies, what are we, where are we, in comparison with populous and growing nations like the United States, Russia, and Germany? With these great Powers, not ignoring France, it is desirable, for the peace and progress of the world, that the British Empire should be on friendly terms and in alliance. This we can best attain and maintain by entering into the relationship on a footing, with respect to population and power, which severance from the Colonies would put out of the question.

The equality and equity of which I speak, of course imply that each of the associated countries which constitute the Empire should subject itself, in respect to Imperial interests, to a central conjoint Administration, which should have the right to determine and legislate for peace or war, emigration and crown lands, and contributions of men and money for military and naval defence and armaments on the basis of population. Allow one remark more. When the Government and Parliament of the United Kingdom made over to their Canadian, Australasian, and African fellow-subjects the control or proprietorship of our magnificent heritage of vast and valuable unoccupied territories, neither contemplated that these should be alienated from the Empire, to whose whole people they belonged, and I trust, for the credit of British rulers and the good of the entire nation, will belong.

I have already suggested that the present juncture, when public attention is earnestly turned to the necessity of reviewing our system of defence and armaments, affords a ready occasion for a convention of delegates from the more important Colonies, to consider that and other cognate questions. I am sure I rightly interpret the general sentiment and wish when I most respectfully express hope that the step will be early taken by the Government. The great work you have accomplished on behalf of Ireland would be dwarfed by success in the not urgent and not less hopeful work which, I trust, you will have the gratification to begin and complete—the strengthening, uniting, and consolidating this noble and royal Empire by an expanded Constitution.—I have the honour to be, &c.

THE HOME GOVERNMENT AND THE COLONIES.

To the Editor of the Times.

Sir,—The loyalty of the Colonists has shown forth, as it was sure to do, since the possibility of the Mother Country being involved in a Continental war became known to them. Will you allow me to occupy a part of your columns with short extracts from the latest Australian newspapers, which show that loyalty, and further indicate expectations and claims deserving earnest heed?

The *Melbourne Argus* of September 18 says:—

We share in the jealous affection which is cherished for the Mother Country by her children in all parts of the world. Her greatness is our greatness, her honour is our honour, her glory is our glory. We neither separate ourselves from her past history nor from her future fortune. . . . In the presence of a common danger men feel how much stronger are the ties of kindred, the instincts of race, and the traditions and renown of a venerable Empire as motive force than the theories of closet philosophers or the doctrines of social parasites. . . . In the whole of these Colonies the Governments and the peoples have obeyed one impulse, and acknowledged one duty to be paramount over all others—that of maintaining the unity of the Empire, and defending ourselves against any enemy with whom England may engage in warfare. . . . If, happily, the storm shall blow over, and England shall maintain undisturbed her pacific relations with the other Great Powers, the precautions which have been forced upon us will not have been without their beneficial uses. We shall have been admonished of the duties which are annexed to the privilege of forming part of a great Empire, and we shall show the Mother Country with what cheerfulness we accept and discharge those duties. Nor must we omit to remind her of the reciprocal obligations which she owes to us.

These obligations are defined to be, along with defence of her territories, "maintaining her naval supremacy," and keeping "the silent highway" of the ocean "clear from all marauders."

The *Melbourne Age* of the same date speaks thus boldly and sensibly :—

A country which is liable to be warred upon must of necessity have the right to make peace. . . . The question we have raised will force itself upon the attention of the party in England which advocates the maintenance of the integrity of the Empire, as well as upon that which disavows all responsibility of the Parent State for its offshoots. It is impossible that the Colonists can remain content to be subjected to all the horrors and disabilities of war without a voice for or against its declaration. . . . The Empire cannot be held together in a state of semi-dislocation. The Colonies must either be integral parts of the Empire, or they must be free in all things. In the meantime we will do our duty as British subjects, in the full hope that we shall not be looked upon and treated as subjects of an inferior grade, burdened with responsibility, but denied the possession of their corresponding rights.

So much for the Southern Hemisphere. Let us look to the Northern. The *Montreal Gazette* of the 1st inst. begins its leader thus :—

It is well sometimes to glance away from interests of merely local value over the immense area which in every region of the world makes the sum total of that mighty Empire of which we form a part. To compare ourselves with our separated brethren of common allegiance, and to compare the British Empire with the other Great Powers of the world, is always instructive and often necessary. . . She (England) is, in fact, much stronger than some of her statesmen seem to consider. The aggregate in extent of territory, in population, and wealth of her foreign Possessions throws into the shade the Empire of Rome in its highest glory. . . . That such an Empire should be disintegrated and destroyed; that the triumphs and trophies of centuries should be made a prey for the first adventurer; that the Colonies won for England long ago by the bravest and settled by the hardiest of her sons, should now, when they are just beginning to be a source of benefit as well as honour, be thrown aside as useless—this is a policy which it is hard to believe that any British statesman should be found to sanction. The danger, however, is now overpast, and there is no longer any fear of so ill-omened an event as the dismemberment of our British household.

The article thus closes:—

> The prosperity of one is the prosperity of all, and in the loving regard of all for each other and for the Motherland, lie the safety, glory, and prosperity of the Empire.

These extracts allude to a "party" which "disavows all responsibility of the Parent State for its offshoots," and to a "policy" that would throw the Colonies aside as useless. There is, we know, really no such party, no such policy, whatever individuals of some position may have said, or been supposed to say. But words have, no longer ago than the last Session of Parliament, been spoken which are not without danger. Even the Prime Minister gave forth the following:—

> There ought to be nothing to preclude the hope, when the growth of a Colonial Possession is such as to make separation from the Mother Country a natural and beneficial result, that that separation, so far from being effected by violence and bloodshed, might be the result of a peaceful and friendly transaction. Surely it is a great object to place, if possible, our Colonial policy on such a footing, not for the purpose of bringing about a separation, but of providing a guarantee that, if separation should occur, it should be in a friendly way. That is the sense, the principle, and the secret of our policy.

He, I am glad to say, added:—

> Our policy gives the best chance of an indefinitely long continuance of a free and voluntary connexion.

So the Under-Secretary of State for the Colonies,

strangely ignoring the strong ties of duty and allegiance, said of the Colonies :—

> They are bound to us by no cords but those of affection and of interest. . . . The desire of Her Majesty's Government, and, he believed, of every party in the State, is . . . to make the ties that bind us so elastic that they may not burst.

It is safe to interpret these regrettable declarations in the light of the recent *Edinburgh Review* article, which, after some obscure expressions, proceeds thus :—

> As regards our Colonies, we have gradually reached the invaluable knowledge that one and the same secret of a free autonomy is a specific alike for the relief of the Mother Country, the masculine and vigorous well-being of the Dependency, and the integrity of the Empire.

The last fortnight has furnished most cogent arguments for some movement on the part of our rulers to direct and employ the loyalty and strength that these extracts recognize, and to endeavour to knit the Empire together in harmony with actual circumstances and wants.

It is obvious that no time should be lost. There are individuals at work to accomplish severance from the Mother Country. Even Dr. Lang, to whom Australia owes much, has published a book with the following unpleasant and ominous title—" The Coming Event ; or, Freedom and Independence for the Seven United Provinces of Australia." Happily a State may be free and independent while federated. The Mother Country desires no less worthy foundation of the Empire. Such consolidation will be strength. Separation would be weakness, all the more to be deprecated when other Great Powers are yearly becoming stronger.

I have suggested that the Secretary of State for the Colonies, speaking in the name of the Queen, should invite the more important Colonies to commission deputies to confer together in London on the best means of defending the Empire and promoting its security, power, and union. The subject of federal connexion would, of course, arise. Much may be said in its favour; but I have occupied so much space already that it is better I should merely mention it.

I am, &c.

Ashfield Hall, *Nov.* 25.

The subsequent mail brought the following. It is from the *Wellington Independent*, but expresses a view not generally entertained, I hope, in the now contented and satisfied Colony of New Zealand:—

Engaged herself in a costly war, Britain will not be able to render great assistance to her Colonies. The question of our independence, therefore, is absolutely forced upon us. If Britain, by her new Colonial policy, has ceased to be great, we must terminate a connexion that is no longer glorious or safe. We cannot shut our eyes to the fact that the Colonial question, from a question of Empire, has dwindled down into a mere question of money. The noble and patriotic and colonizing principles which rendered Britain what she is are now no more in the ascendant. We will have to face this question sooner or later. Can there be a better time than the present, when our danger is imminent, and there is yet time to avert it? If our connexion is to be severed, let it be done deliberately and not hastily, in a time of peace and not of war. Let us part (if part we must) as friends, submitting to a deplorable necessity, and not as discontented children from churlish parents. We do not wish to raise unnecessary alarm, but the probability of Britain being forced into war cannot be disregarded. In such a case, our ports would be liable to blockade, our towns to plunder; our exports of wool, flax, and gold might be seized by cruisers; and all the evils of a war, in which we have no interest, might be on us before we are aware. We should now, therefore, put our case before the Imperial Government, and ask them—if they cannot give us sufficient protection, or diplomatic arrangements to have the law of nations so revised as to make Colonial flags neutral—to free us at once, by some treaty of Independence or otherwise, from a connexion which is a source of danger to us as it is of weakness to them. They have invited us to depart; let us now amicably settle the terms and go in peace.

The subjoined extract from the Report of the Commission appointed by the Governor of Victoria, is in the same strain:—

The British Colonies from which Imperial troops have been wholly withdrawn present the unprecedented phenomenon of responsibility without either corresponding authority or adequate protection. They are liable to all the hazards of war as the United Kingdom; but they influence the commencememt or continuance of a war no more than they can control the movements of the solar system; and they have no certain assurance of that aid against an enemy upon which integral portions of the United Kingdom can confidently reckon. This is a relation so wanting in mutuality that it cannot safely be regarded as a lasting one, and it becomes necessary to consider how it may be so modified as to afford a greater security for permanence.

In an article on the British Army, the October *Quarterly Review* quotes a private letter from Quebec, which says:—

The removal of the troops—the general neglect—is the moving cause. Everywhere the cry is "Independence!" I have not yet talked with one man who is in favour of remaining *in statu quo*.

The *Pall Mall Gazette*, of December 14, says of the Canadian *Dominion*:—

Strong as her affection is for this country, she conceals it wonderfully.

Perhaps so; but we on our side have somewhat dissembled our love! We are not even Platonic. We have, by approving of the ambitious name Dominion, sanctioned a certain coolness. I have before me *The Government Gazette Extraordinary, British Columbia*, of August 30. It contains a despatch from the Governor-General of Canada, and a Report of the committee of the Privy Council of Canada, arranging the union of that Province with Canada, in neither of which documents do I find the smallest mention of the Queen and Mother Country, except the following :—

in the former—

The Hon Mr. Trutch goes to England, &c.

I announced the result of the negotiations, and sent a copy of the memorandum to Lord Granville on the 5th inst.

in the latter :—

6. Suitable pensions, such as shall be approved by Her Majesty's Government . . . for those of Her Majesty's servants in the Colony whose position . . . would be affected, &c.

13. . . . In case of disagreement between the two Governments [respecting land for Indians], the matter shall be referred for the decision of the Secretary of State for the Colonies.

The Union shall take effect, according to the foregoing terms and conditions, on such day as Her Majesty, by and with the advice of the Most Honourable Privy Council, may appoint (on addresses from the Legislature of the Colonies of British Columbia, and of the Houses of Parliament of Canada), &c.

COLONIAL DEFENCES.

The foregoing Letter produced, some days after, the following from Captain J. C. R. Colomb :—

To the Editor of the Times.

SIR,—The letter of Mr. Macfie, M.P., on the " Home Government and the Colonies," is a striking addendum to my first letter on " Imperial Strategy," in which I pointed out that national defence involves the defence of the United Kingdom, the occupation of India, and the protection of our commerce or communications. I now crave a small space to expose myself to the charge of egotism by quoting a few brief extracts from lectures on the " Distribution of our War Forces," delivered by me before the Royal United Service Institution, which deals with that part of the question so forcibly alluded to by Mr. Macfie—viz., the Defence of the Colonies :—

"I think it may fairly be assumed that in the matter of National Defence we are bound to look to the general welfare of the Empire, but when we remember the vast extent of our territories, scattered as they are over the face of the globe, it is manifestly impossible to take the whole burden of their defence upon our own shoulders. It is reasonable to say that those Colonies and Dependencies whose geographical position and natural advantages do not entitle them to be considered as military positions necessary for the general safety of the Empire, must defend themselves. There are many places which, for the sake of our communications, we must strain every nerve to hold against all odds, but to the rest of our Possessions we are compelled by limited means to say, 'Defend yourselves from direct attack; we can do no more than guard the communications which are common to us all.' We should say this because it is useless and wrong to hold out hopes of military assistance which in their hour of danger we should have to withdraw, and it is evident that if we can secure these highroads to ourselves, and consequently to them, they would, with the sole exception of Canada, be virtually excluded from the possibility of attack."

Then, having argued against holding Canada by defending its frontier with British troops, I said :—

"By all means, in peace and war, let us give to our North American Provinces, and to all our other dominions, all the assistance we can in the shape of experienced officers and military equipment, but do not let us risk our regular forces in the direct defence of any portion of our territory the possession of which is not essentially necessary to the safety of the State. Let us guard against the military blunder of leaving our communications and our whole position exposed in order to defend small and, in a purely military sense, valueless posts. Let Canada, and all our Colonies and territories unnecessary to the Empire as military posts, fully and clearly understand that we will never suffer them to be wrested from the Mother Country; that any attempt to do so will bring down upon the aggressor the vengeance of England, but that they must rely on themselves for protection from direct assault, in order to leave the regular forces of the United Kingdom free to act in such a manner as will best make that vengeance felt."

"The communications of the Empire being the common property of all its component parts, it follows that their security is an imperial necessity, and that our first duty towards our Colonies and Possessions is to provide means by which the roads between us and them may be kept open. For this purpose the fleet is, of course, the engine to employ; but, in order to enable it to act, it must be divided into parts, these being distributed in different quarters of the globe, the strength of each part being in proportion to the forces against which it would probably have to contend, and to the interests it has to protect. As each fleet constantly requires stores, repairs, and reserves of men, the protection of our communications would not be accomplished by the judicious distribution of the Navy, unless means are devised for securing to each fleet the power of self-support; therefore each must be provided with a head-quarters, or base of operations, where all these things, so essential to its vigorous action, are to be found."

I then proceeded to state that these minor bases should be situated so as to command the lines of communication and possess natural advantages rendering them capable of defence, and of being not only depôts for war forces, but also ports of refuge for our traders during maritime war; the naval stations, of which they are respectively the head-quarters, being so arranged as to make them central points, they should be, further, the chief, if not the only, coaling ports of the stations.

According to my calculation, they are 16 in number, including Bombay, which is the natural grand base of operations in the Eastern seas. They would all require garrisons in time of maritime war. They are, Sir, the "strategic points" which we must strain every nerve to hold.

Having named them, and the means necessary for their defence, I concluded by saying:—

"It has been truly stated that it is wiser to concentrate the resources of a country on the fortifications of the principal arsenals, so as to secure them against capture, than to expend the same resources on many comparatively unimportant points, which, from their isolation and weakness, invite attack and afford cheap victories. Now, viewing the whole Empire as a country exposed to attack, it may be said that it would be better to turn our resources to the purpose of securing points which command our communications than to fritter them away in attempting to defend a variety of unimportant positions. How far we have hitherto acted upon this principle may be gathered from the fact that the estimated Imperial military expenditure upon our Colonies and Dependencies for the year 1864-5 amounted to about 3,500,000*l.*, and of this sum only about 1,300,000*l.* was expended on the outposts I have named. Now, if these positions are lost to us, the safety of our communications is gone. That being the case, we could do little to assist any of our distant Possessions in time of need. Why, then, expend nearly two-thirds of our available resources upon unimportant points, which would afford 'cheap victories,' while but one-third is spent upon positions the loss of which would involve the whole Empire in a state of commercial and military paralysis?"

If, Sir, Mr. Macfie's proposal for a commission of deputies to confer on the best means of defending the Empire be carried into effect, it will be a curious practical comment on words put forward by me anonymously four years ago in "the protection of our commerce." When speaking of the Defence Commission of 1859 these words occur :—

"It is to be regretted that the labours of the Commissioners were confined to the question of invasion alone. A consideration of the means to be adopted for national defence can only be based upon national requirement, and cannot be limited to drawing up designs for improving the fortifications of our dockyards and arsenals at home, which, after all, is but a matter of detail in the general scheme for the safety of the Empire."

I am, &c.

OPINIONS OF THE AUTHOR OF "FRIENDS IN COUNCIL."

(From *Good Words* for December, 1870.)

"I now proceed to discuss the third branch of the subject—namely, the relation of the Colony to the Parent State.

"There are five different conditions of this relation. . . .

"2. Then there is that condition of a Colony which is complete in its union with the Parent State—when the difference between the Colonist and the Citizen at home is a difference of distance only from the centre of government. There are few, if any, perfect instances of this condition of a Colony; but I would wish to impress upon the reader that there is no reason in the nature of things why this condition could not be originated and maintained. Modern ways and means all tend to render it more feasible. The swiftness of communication and the general assimilation of manners and habits in modern times are greatly in its favour. Probably, had it been more tried, it would have had more to say for itself. I will hereafter return to a further consideration of it. . . . .

"4. There is the condition of federation. Now federation may be of two kinds. There is the federation which exists only for the purposes of war, or, to put it more largely, for the purposes of dealing with foreign States. Again, there is the federation which is of a much more intimate kind, and such as that which prevails among the respective States of the great American Republic—a federation in which a certain community of law, privilege, and citizenship exists, and in which the several communities are knit together by common principles of thought and action. These communities may, or may not, have a central seat of government. The principle of federation is the same in both cases.

"Even the minor experiment has not been tried, of attaching a Council to the Colonial Office, composed of eminent Colonists returning to the Mother Country for a certain period, or of persons who have distinguished themselve in colonization, or of those who are versed in the study of the Colonies and Colonial administration. We have a similar body connected with the affairs of India; but we have never given to our Colonial administration the aid and security which such a Council would afford."

CLIPPINGS FROM DR. LANG'S NEW BOOK.

[*The italics are in the original.*]

I have now received a copy of this goodly octavo of more than 500 pages. It is not my part to criticise it, nor to expose its weaknesses. I met Dr. Lang a third of a century ago. He was an eminent Colonist then, and must now be far advanced in years, and I have been accustomed to hold him in respect. He has the good of Australia at heart. I regret that he allows his feelings such vent as to make the reading of the book painful. In spite of questionable logic and consistency—for the composition is crude and not homogeneous—it is instructive and suggestive. The Doctor proves successfully that the *status quo* of the Colonial relations is utterly unsatisfactory, and he makes many admissions, and adduces not a few arguments and quotations, for which he deserves thanks. To a certain extent he and we go together. Perhaps he would cheerfully halt where we stop. This is the more probable, as among the schemes which he combats, the rational one of an Imperial Confederation finds no place. He strangely ignores it throughout, and does not even approach it except in one case, where he seems to introduce it unconsciously, and, as will be seen below, mistakes what is meant.

In the Dedication his aim is stated, in connexion with bold assertions, thus:—

" The settlement of the great question that is now virtually submitted for our decision—viz., as to whether we and the Colonies to the northward are to remain for an indefinite period mere Colonies of Britain, or to assume the noble position of a Sovereign and Independent State on the Pacific Ocean, with a territory extending from Cape Howe to Cape York, and the city of Sydney for its capital, as the Queen of the Isles of the Western Pacific.

" You will see from this volume that it is the law of nature and the ordinance of God, that full-grown Colonies, like ourselves, should assume such a position as I have indicated at the earliest possible period, *for the benefit of their Mother Country, as well as for their own.*

" You will also see that from Great Britain's ignoring, or rather wilfully shutting her eyes to this great fact, her colonization system for the last two hundred and fifty years—so far from meriting the praise which ignorance and self-glorification have so often bestowed upon it—has been nothing less than an enormous political blunder, an offence of very serious magnitude in the eyes of Heaven, and a loss of incalculable amount, not only to herself and her Colonies, but to the human race.

" You will likewise see that the Mother Country, tacitly recognizing this great political blunder of the past, has at length expressed her willingness that we should at once assume such a position as I have indicated, and has intimated her meaning in the matter in the most significant manner, by the withdrawal of her troops from all these Australian Colonies.

" You will see, moreover, that there is an urgent necessity at present for our immediately taking the step I have recommended, from the critical state of things in the rich and beautiful Isles of the Western Pacific, that naturally look to us as their guide and protector.

" And you will see finally that by assuming the high and highly influential position that thus awaits us—by taking our place at once in the family of nations, with the entire concurrence of Her Majesty's Government—we may be the means of relieving our beloved Mother Country, in a comparatively short period, of not less perhaps than half a million of her redundant population, without expense either to herself or to us, and planting them as British Colonists in the multitude of the Isles."

Again, in the Preface:—

" It is the primary object of the following work to point out the right principles of colonization, and to confirm the theory thus advanced by an appeal to the principles and practice of those nations, both in ancient and modern times, whose efforts in the work of colonization have not only been successful, but have, notwithstanding all our boasting on the subject, presented a perfect contrast with our own. In short, it is the object of the writer to show that Great Britain has hitherto been all wrong in her principles and practice in the matter of colonization, and to point out, in accordance with the laws of nature and the ordinance of God, a more excellent way ; that way being the way of entire freedom and independence. . . .

" While this volume was passing through the press, an Intercolonial Conference was held in Melbourne, with a view to take into consideration the practicability and the propriety of establishing a General

Customs League and a uniform tariff for all the Australian Colonies —preparatory, as such a measure was conceived to be, to a general federation of the Colonies. In the prospect of this most desirable consummation, the writer had perhaps too confidently urged the claim for freedom and independence for the Seven United Provinces of Australia. But the result of that Conference has shown that is hopeless to expect an incorporating union of all the Seven Provinces at present; the three Colonies on Bass's Straits and the Great Southern Ocean—viz., Victoria, Tasmania, and South Australia—being banded together in favour of Protective Duties; while New South Wales, the oldest of the group and the mother of all the rest, adheres firmly to the system of Free Trade. It has, therefore, become necessary to leave out of the programme the three Southern Colonies, for the present at least, and to confine the claim of freedom and independence to the Colonies, both present and prospective, on the Pacific Ocean, from Cape Howe to Cape York—viz., New South Wales, Queensland, Capricornia, and Carpentaria.

"The principal reason for urging the immediate accomplishment of the great object in view is the absolute necessity for the erection of a Sovereign and Independent Power on the Pacific, in view of the actual state of things in the Fiji Islands. On this transcendently important subject, however, it is pitiful to think that the Conference could only come to the following impotent conclusion:—

" BRITISH PROTECTORATE OVER FIJI.

" ' This Conference, being of opinion that the geographical position of the Fiji Islands renders their protection of the very highest consideration as regards Australia, and both British and Australian commerce,—

" ' Resolves,—That it is of the utmost importance to British interests that these islands should not form part of or be under the guardianship of any other country than Great Britain; and that a respectful address to this effect be prepared for transmission to the Imperial authorities.'

"Did the Conference really suppose that, after their recent declaration in behalf of Colonial freedom, and their recent and still more significant proceedings, in withdrawing the Imperial troops from the Australian Colonies and New Zealand, Her Majesty's Government could possibly stultify itself by assuming the responsibility of establishing a British Protectorate over the Fiji Islands, and thereby incurring the risk of another war with savages in the Pacific Ocean?

There are at present upwards of two thousand white men, chiefly British, with about one-third Americans and Germans, in the Fiji Islands; and the native population is estimated at two hundred thousand. There is actually at this moment also a requisition in Sydney from the Islands to prohibit the export of fire-arms for the use of the natives—which, however, cannot be done without an Act of Parliament, and the report of which will certainly not induce Her Majesty's Government to change their minds or to move in the matter, after their bitter recollections of New Zealand. On the other hand, there are people in these Islands actually talking still about annexation to the United States or to the North German Confederation. In such circumstances, there is an evident and urgent necessity for action of some kind in the matter; and earnestly desirous as the writer is, in common with the Intercolonial Conference, that the Fiji Islands may never fall under the guardianship of any foreign Power, it must be evident that the only way in which this can be prevented, and a really British Protectorate over these Islands established, is the one recommended in this volume—that of erecting a Sovereign and Independent State on the Pacific."

The first sentence of the Work itself defines a Colony to be "a body of people who have gone forth from the Parent State, either simultaneously or progressively, and formed a permanent settlement in some remote territory." He omits from the definition the idea that the land on which the Colony settles belonged to the Mother Country, and continues a part of the national territories. Is it *fair* to assume that they have *left* the Parent State? Mark the covert insinuation!

He is careful in distinguishing between the *people*, whom he recognizes as the Colony, and the *province*, or territory on which they settle. It is in the latter sense we speak of "the British Colonies."

" It is a common but an unfounded idea that the word Colony has a territorial meaning, and signifies the tract of country inhabited, or to be inhabited, by any body of Colonists, as well as the people who form the Colony. It has no such meaning, however. It signifies the people exclusively. . . . This mistake, as to the meaning of the word Colony, has been rather a serious matter to Colonists generally; for by taking it for granted that a particular nation has rights, arising either from discovery or conquest, over a particular unoccupied territory or Colony, in the territorial sense of the word, it has been inferred, without the least shadow of reason, that it has also a right to govern the people who may settle within that territory for all time coming. Now we Colonists admit the national right, whether of discovery or of conquest, as a right against any other colonizing nation; but we repudiate the inference of its implying a right to govern the future occupants of the territory, as being altogether unfounded in reason and justice. For example, we admit the right of Great Britain to the exclusive colonization of the whole east coast of Australia, that coast having been discovered, in the interest and on behalf of the British nation, by our illustrious fellow-countryman, Captain Cook; and we would therefore do our best, as Britons, to prevent any other European nation from forming settlements on that coast. But we maintain, as Australian Colonists, that this right of discovery, as well as of exclusive colonization in favour of Great Britain, which it implies, implies no right whatever, on the part of the British people, to exercise domination over the British Colonists who may settle from time to time on that coast. . . .

"Our definition must also exclude such Dependencies of the British Empire as Lower Canada, the Mauritius, St. Lucia, the Cape of Good Hope, Demerara, and Trinidad. . .

"Neither are the really British Islands of the West Indies—Jamaica, Barbadoes, St. Vincent, &c., including the Bahama Islands—entitled to be called *British* Colonies. At least nine out of every ten of the inhabitants of these Islands are Africans or the descendants of Africans, who were originally stolen from their native country and made slaves of, to grow, sugar, cotton, and coffee for Englishmen; and the very few Britons, comparatively, who ever went to them went merely to make money, and *to return*. These Islands are therefore merely British Possessions. . . .

"They are all British Possessions, and it is doubtless necessary for the purposes of a great maritime and commercial nation that they should always remain so; but not one of them is a *British Colony*, properly so called. . .

"Still less are we entitled to profane the designation *British Colony* —which I confess I consider a very high and honourable distinction for any community, and one that ought not to be lightly applied or appropriated where it is not deserved—by applying to any of those numerous posts or stations that are held either for naval and military purposes, or for the furtherance and protection of commerce."

The venerable author proceeds to the objects of colonization:—

"What then are the proper and legitimate objects which such a country as Great Britain ought to have in view or to propose to herself in forming such Colonies as these—British Colonies properly so called? They are—

" 1. To secure an eligible outlet for her redundant population of all grades and classes.

" 2. To create a market for her manufactured produce by increasing and multiplying its consumers indefinitely.

" 3. To open up a field for the growth of raw produce for her trade and manufactures ; and,

" 4. To sustain and extend her commerce by carrying out all these objects simultaneously.

" Now these are noble objects for any nation to pursue ; and no wonder that Lord Bacon should designate the peculiar work they indicate *the heroic work* of colonization. Nay, it is something more even than a merely heroic work : it is the course divinely prescribed in the first commandment given to the human race, " *Be fruitful and multiply, and replenish the earth, and subdue it ;* " and it may, therefore, be inferred that it can never be safe for any nation to neglect this work, if in the peculiar circumstances to which the commandment applies. For, as " *God made the earth to be inhabited,*" He will certainly hold that nation which he has specially called in His Providence to carry out this Divine ordinance, responsible for the neglect of its proper duty, if it has been neglected, and will afflict and punish it accordingly. . . .

" It must be clear therefore as daylight that Great Britain has been specially called, in the good Providence of God, to the *heroic* work of colonization. She has by far the largest Colonial Empire in the world : she has facilities for colonization such as no other nation on earth has ever had since the foundation of the world ; and she has a remarkably redundant, and at the same time a peculiarly energetic people, the fittest on earth for this heroic work, and the most willing to engage in it heartily. And it must be equally clear, from our very limited experience on the subject as a colonizing nation, that a regular and systematic obedience of the Divine commandment, on the part of Great Britain, would, in such circumstances, enable her to realize all the objects of colonization enumerated above."

The reader will please observe that among the objects of colonization, and therefore of retention of colonies, preservation and increase of the nation's power is not mentioned.

The Preface begins thus :—

" There is no great public question in which the British nation has so deep an interest, or in regard to which a large proportion of the intelligence of the country is so profoundly and fatally ignorant, as the Colonial question, or the proper relation of a Mother Country to her Colonies."

He allows elsewhere—

" It is one of the gratifying signs of the times that the true relation of a Colony to its Mother Country is thus at length understood and appreciated in the most influential quarters, both at home and abroad."

Heavy as are his discharges of artillery against the departed system of Colonial government, he always honourably acknowledges that all is changed now.

In page 8 in the Preface he speaks of

" The bad system of government that has universally prevailed, till very recently, in the British Colonies."

Again:

" The last state of the British Colonies, till the advent of responsible government in the year 1856, has been worse than the first."

Nevertheless, Dr. Lang argues persistently that the relations of the Colonies with the United Kingdom are not on a right footing. It domineers over them. It is chargeable with lust of empire (meaning *imperium*, rule, no doubt). They are of age, and should be free and independent. They aspire to become Colonial nationalities. He asks, " What right can either Her Majesty Queen Victoria, or the Imperial Parliament, have to subject us to their dominion one hour longer than we please ourselves ? . . .

" As to the charge of our violating or renouncing our allegiance to Her Majesty the Queen, in claiming, as we do, our entire freedom and independence, I repeat it, there is *a previous question* to be put and answered, ere this knotty point can be determined, ere this offensive charge can be substantiated—I mean the question as to whether we, as British Colonists who have attained our political majority, have, or have not, a right to our entire freedom and independence. For if we have such a right, as I have shown we have, the right of Her Majesty the Queen to reign over us necessarily ceases and determines. Under the universal government of God there cannot possibly be two inconsistent and incompatible rights; and the right to obedience or allegiance, on the one part, is clearly inconsistent and incompatible with the right to freedom and independence on the other. . . . Let us hear no more, then, of this pitiful, this contemptible charge, about our violating or renouncing our allegiance. The question is, do we *owe* such allegiance, in the sense in which the term is used in the charge, as implying that we have no rights in the case? To which I unhesitatingly answer, No."

Who will call that loyal?

" There is a time when the youth is no longer to be *under tutors and governors.* He attains his majority." . . .

" There is certainly no law requiring a young man to claim entire freedom from all parental control when he attains his majority; and if he chooses to remain in his father's house, and assist him in his business, that is his own affair, and is supposed to be matter of private arrangement between his father and himself, with which no law can interfere." . .

" As time wears on, and the new interests with which he has become identified are multiplied and strengthened, this feeling gradually ripens into a spirit of what may perhaps be designated *Colonial nationality.* His native land gradually fades from his view, and his interest in its peculiar objects becomes fainter and fainter. The particular Colony, or group of Colonies, to which he belongs, engrosses all his affections.

" So far indeed from the feeling of nationality being a mere matter of the imagination, it constitutes a bond of brotherhood of the most influential and salutary character, and forms one of the most powerful principles of virtuous action. Like the main-spring of a watch, it sets the whole machinery in motion. Like the heart, it causes the pulse of life to beat in the farthest extremities of the system. It is the very soul of society, which animates and exalts the whole brotherhood of associated men.". . . .

On the foregoing I make only these remarks. As already shown, the " young man " is partner in a firm holding valuable properties. His coming of age does not entitle him to carry these off. Seeing the principle of nationality is so good, why cause the national relationship already constituted and implied to cease?

" Must it be held a crime for the Australian Colonist, who has come forth in the vigour of manhood to this far land, to labour earnestly for the freedom and independence of his adopted country, and to identify himself, in reality as well as in imagination, with the coming glories of that great nation of the future of which he forms a part?"

"In one word, nationality, or their entire freedom and independence, is absolutely necessary for the social welfare and political advancement of the Australian Colonies. Give us *this*, and you give us everything to enable us to become a great and glorious people. Withhold *this*, and you give us nothing." . . .

"With all his acuteness, Mr. Wakefield has confounded two things that are essentially distinct from each other, viz., 'the love of England,' and the 'love of her Empire,' or Government, in the sense of a strong desire to be, or to continue, under it. The love of England—meaning the love of the country, of its people, of its institutions, and of its prosperity—is a generous and manly feeling, which, I am most happy to admit with Mr. Wakefield, is the characteristic of *all British Colonies;* and so far from there being anything either strange or unaccountable in it, as Mr. W. seems to imagine, it is the most natural thing in the world. For, according to the Scotch proverb, 'Blood is thicker than water,' or, in other words, 'we shall always be more kindly-affectioned towards our *own* kindred, our *own* country, our *own* race, than towards mere strangers or foreigners,' *provided always that no disturbing element shall have intervened,* as in the case of the War of Independence in America."

"But Mr. Wakefield is decidedly in the wrong in taking it for granted, as he does, that this love of England, which is both natural and universal in British Colonies, necessarily implies a desire to live under her *Government,* as mere Dependencies of her Empire."

Be it so. Why not welcome the proposition which is ready to be entertained, of a new system founded on the principle of "Liberty, Fraternity, and *Equality?*" England does not wish to *govern* nor *dominate,* if a better practical system is exhibited and its adoption desired.

"There is *a previous question* to be answered—viz., 'Is the extension of the Empire of the Mother Country compatible with the attainment of the other and legitimate ends of colonization?' And this is a question I have no hesitation in answering in the negative—it is not." . . .

There is a general hope and impression that the system of Confederation will remove these disadvantages. May not this have been in Dr. Lang's mind when he wrote as follows:—

"The disadvantages in question arise principally from the ignorance and indifference of the dominant country about the position and interests of the Dependency. . . .

"There is, I firmly believe, a career of national greatness and glory for Great Britain, in friendly alliance and co-operation with Australia —free and independent—such as her most sanguine orators and poets have never imagined."

As an inducement for Britain to listen to his counsels, we read:—

"It is as like a universal Empire as possible, *and therefore the more likely to be dismembered, as it is called, very shortly.* For Divine Providence has, for the last thirteen hundred and fifty years—that is, ever since the Roman Empire, or fourth universal monarchy, fell—set its face against the establishment of anything like another universal Empire or fifth monarchy upon earth; consequently, the more extensive any Empire becomes, and the more closely it approaches to universality, we have every reason to believe that it is only the nearer its fall or dismemberment." . . .

"Now it appears to me that we are approaching a somewhat similar crisis in the history of the British Empire at the present moment. For a long time past we have been adding province to province in India, till our Empire in that country now comprises a hundred and eighty millions of people—about an eighth part of the whole human race! We have also been adding province to province in Africa. We have humbled China, and planted a Colony, as we call it by courtesy, and a line of posts on her frontier. We have annexed New Zealand to our Australasian Dominion; and we have added Aden, Singapore, and Labuan, to our Empire in the East; and certain political enthusiasts in the Colonies are actually promising us the whole multitude of the Isles of the vast Pacific. In short, never was the British Empire more extensive than it is at present; never was its power more formidable, in every land and on every sea. The press everywhere is telling us, *usque ad nauseam*, that the sun never sets upon it, and a certain idolatrous limner at the first Great Exhibition, catching the vain-glorious spirit of the age, actually represented the four quarters of the globe paying homage to Queen Victoria."

"Now no man of the slightest discernment can be blind to these very significant signs of the times. Such national pride, accompanied as it is with such national dereliction of duty towards the poor in the land, for whom this vast Colonial Empire is held in trust, necessarily precedes a fall; for it cannot but be peculiarly offensive in the eyes of the Great Governor among the nations. We are evidently hastening to another great crisis in the history of our country. We are on the eve of another dismemberment ; and I shall be greatly mistaken if, in a very few years hence, both the Eastern Colonies of Australia and the British Colonies of North America shall not have ceased to belong to the British Empire. Which of 'the two great groups will go first, no man can tell ; but it is certain, at all events, that they are both getting ready."

"And why should they not? And why should a great nation like ours seek to prevent them? If it is the right of these groups of Colonies, by the law of nature and the ordinance of God, to form two great nations, instead of a series of miserable and till very lately miserably-governed Dependencies, and to assume the prominent and highly influential position they are destined to occupy in that capacity on the face of the earth, why should Englishmen endeavour, in their folly and madness, either to prevent or to postpone 'a consummation so devoutly to be wished ?' "

Fervently I trust that the allegations contained in the following paragraphs are unwarranted. I am aware that they are not without seeming foundation. Taking them at the strongest, no Government has authority to promise away the rights of the Queen and people. Parliament has never been consulted. The United Kingdom has not consented. The rest of the nation in the distant Colonies has the same right as ourselves to veto such alienation.

" ' The people of England,' says the leading journal of Europe " [and the passage is thrice quoted in this volume !] " ' have long ago renounced any wish to retain by force of arms remote settlements, inhabited by people of our own race, in unwilling and compulsory subjection. Henceforth the bond of union which unites Britain to her Colonies must be free.' And the Imperial Government of the present day have nobly endorsed these enlightened and patriotic sentiments, by telling us, in so many words, that if the Australian Colonies really desire their entire freedom and independence, Her Majesty's Government will not stand in their way. Leaving therefore the case of New Zealand for further consideration in the sequel, Her Majesty's Government have distinctly intimated to the authorities of the Colonies generally, on issuing the recent orders for the withdrawal of the troops (which, it must be confessed, have been stationed in these Australian Colonies for years past rather for ornament than for use), that if this or any other group of Colonies should desire to be separated from the Mother

Country, and to become an independent nationality or nationalities, Her Majesty's Government would leave them entire liberty of action in the matter, and would not oppose their desire in any way."

"'The people of England,' says the leading journal of Europe, in a passage I have already quoted above, 'have long ago renounced any wish to retain by force of arms remote settlements, inhabited by people of our own race, in unwilling and compulsory subjection. Henceforth the bond of union which unites Britain to her Colonies must be free."

"The Australian Colonies will therefore have no need of a second Washington to achieve their freedom and independence; and still less will they stand in need of another La Fayette to assist him. They will only have to signify their desire to become a free, sovereign, and independent State, in real earnest, and the thing will be done without further trouble."

On the contrary, the people, the masses, will be moved with indignation. No Ministry could stand against the storm that would arise.

The illustrations which the author gives of ancient colonization favour his views but little. Here are specimens:—

"And what a difference there must have been in any great effort of colonization in such circumstances as these, from the miserable affair that we call colonization! In the case of the Greeks, men of all ranks in society, of all professions and occupations, went forth on the great undertaking, and staked their character and their fortunes on the issue; but they all went forth from the same mother-city or State, and they were all perfectly acquainted with each other before they started on their noble undertaking. As an embryo community, they had all from the first the same interesting associations, and the same endearing recollections of the land they had left; they had all the same objects and interests, the same feelings and views in the land of their adoption. The sprightly and enterprising Ionian from Athens was not incommoded with the presence of the dull Bœotian from Thebes, or the plodding Dorian from the plain of Argos. Ionians, Æolians, and Dorians had all their separate Colonies; and every Greek emigrant found himself, on his arrival in his adopted country, in the midst of his old neighbours, and countrymen, and friends. They all left the same locality in the *old* country, and they all settled together in the *new*."

"Under our colonization system, people of a certain class only—people who have somehow lost their way in the world—people who have tried everything at home, and have uniformly failed—people who have already reached, or are fast verging towards, the lower walks of life—people of this kind assemble from all quarters of the three kingdoms, and meet together for the first time in some great shipping port, as, for instance, Liverpool. . . . Falling, as they now do, among utter strangers, the moral restraints of their native vicinage are gradually weakened, and perhaps completely lost. . . . *The great bulk of the Greek Colonies were really independent States;* and though they commonly regarded the land of their forefathers with filial respect, though they yielded to its citizens the place of distinction at public games and religious solemnities, and were expected to assist them in time of war, they did so as allies only, on fair and equal terms, and never as subjects. . . . The Grecian Colonists almost uniformly defrayed the expenses of their own emigration and settlement; while the Roman, like the earlier settlers in New South Wales, had grants of land and free passage *out*, with rations and other indulgences, including an ample supply of slave labour, from the State. The lands were held by the leading Colonists on a tenure somewhat similar to that of the feudal system, each large estate being a knight's fee. McCulloch, in his *Dictionary of Commerce*, under the Article 'Colonies,' gives the following account of the Roman Colonies. . . . 'The most intimate political union was always maintained between them and the mother-city. Their internal Government was modelled on that of Rome; and, while their superior officers were mostly sent from the capital, they were made to contribute their full quota of troops and taxes, to assist in carrying on the contests in which the Republic was almost constantly engaged.'"

His deductions from "American Colonization—its Principles and Results." are still more confirmatory of the principle of Imperial Confederation :—

"In a work which I published in 1840, on my return to London from a tour of observation in the United States, entitled 'Religion and Education in America,' I showed that those States and territories of the American Union which have been either acquired or settled since the War of Independence, including the great valley of the Mississippi, bear precisely the same relation to the original Thirteen States as the numerous Colonies of Britain do to the United Kingdom. They are, to all intents and purposes, the Colonies of the United States; for, as far as the relation of a Mother Country and a Colony is concerned, it is of no importance whatever whether the latter is planted on the same Continent or Island as the Mother Country, or is separated from

it by vast tracts of intervening ocean. This idea, I perceive, has since been put forth by John Arthur Roebuck, Esq., in his work entitled 'The Colonies of England,' with a view to contrast the progress and extent of colonization in the United States, with its progress and extent in the British Empire, since the peace of 1783;"
Mr. Roebuck, however, is represented as saying :—

"'The Colony would, in such a case, continue to feel towards the Mother Country with kindness and respect; a close union would exist between them, and all their mutual relations would be so ordered as to conduce to the welfare of both.' . . .

The following extract presents admirable proof of the advantage, the crying call, for a Union of the British Dominions :—

"Surely, then, if the art of colonization has been lost, as it seems to have been, in old England, it has been found again in New England; for I question whether even the ancient Greeks ever surpassed the New Englanders in that noble art, that *heroic work.*

"What then is the reason—for there surely must be some adequate reason—for the prodigious difference in the two results? Why, the answer is plain and obvious to the meanest capacity. America, like the ancient Greeks, gives her Colonies freedom and independence from the first; whereas Great Britain, until a very recent period, uniformly withheld anything like manly freedom from her Colonies, treated them with the coldest neglect and the grossest injustice, and harassed and oppressed them in every possible way with the incubus and the curse of her Colonial Office. Yes; instead of insulting her Colonies by offering them what certain *soi-disant* Colonial reformers in England think it would be a great deal indeed for Great Britain to offer hers—viz., municipal independence—which signifies allowing them to manage for themselves in all little matters, and leaving all important ones to be managed for them at home, or, in other words, the Colonial Office—instead of insulting her Colonies by offering them municipal independence, America gives them at once complete independence; that is, the entire control of all matters affecting their interests, as men and as citizens, in every possible way. In short, America realizes the *beau ideal* which the ancient Locrians indignantly reminded the Corinthians was the implied condition of their own emigration—she makes her Colonies in every respect like herself; she treats her Colonists not as her slaves or subjects, but as her equals."

The following passage is particularly suggestive :—

"Another great point of difference between the future National

Government of Australia and that of the United States is that, whereas the possession and management of the waste lands of the country are vested by the Constitution of the United States in the Federal Government, the waste lands of Australia would in all likelihood remain in the possession and under the exclusive management of the Provincial Parliaments respectively. I cannot see that such a system as that of the United States, in regard to the waste lands of the country, could be adopted with propriety, or even with safety, in Australia. The Provincial Governments would be quite competent to manage the waste lands within their respective boundaries; and I am confident they would never allow the funds accruing either from the management or the sales of these lands to be placed in a common Treasury, like that of the United States, to be divided rateably among the Provinces, according to the population of each, or applied to the general purposes of the National Government."

We now proceed to extracts which show the kind of authorities on which Dr. Lang rests his audacious pretensions. The first quotations are from *Grotius* :—

" An equality of condition cannot subsist between the citizens of the Mother Country and those of the Colonies. It becomes, therefore, just and necessary that the latter should have a suitable compensation for the disadvantages of their situation, and for the re-establishment of the equilibrium. Their liberty, therefore, ought to be augmented in proportion to the distance of the countries they inhabit, and the difficulties that stand in the way of their frequent communication with those among whom the legislative body resides.

" But that very authority ought necessarily to diminish in proportion as the number of the Colonists increases, or be abrogated when their wants cease. Everything, then, re-enters into the imperturbable order of nature; political ties are formed by new conventions, and the rights of government are established on a new basis."

The principle of Adam Smith was :—

" If it was adopted, however, Great Britain would not only be immediately freed from the whole annual expense of the peace establishment of the Colonies, but *might settle with them such a treaty of commerce as would effectually secure her a free trade* more advantageous to the great body of the people, though less so to the merchants, than the monopoly which she at present enjoys. By thus parting good friends, the natural affection of the Colonies to the

Mother Country, which, perhaps, our late dissensions have well-nigh extinguished, would quickly revive. It might dispose them not only to respect, for whole centuries together, that treaty of commerce which they had concluded with us at parting, but to favour us in war as well as in trade, and, instead of turbulent and factious subjects, to become our most faithful, affectionate, and generous allies; and the same sort of parental affection on the one side, and filial respect on the other, might revive between Great Britain and her Colonies, which used to subsist between the Colonies of ancient Greece and the Mother City from which they descended."

"But the world has been making great advances since the days of Adam Smith; for the following generous and enlightened sentiment has appeared (as I have already had occasion to observe) in an article on Australia in the leading journal of Europe, nearly eighteen years ago:—'The people of England,'" &c. [Already quoted twice!]

"'Many,' says the celebrated Dr. Benjamin Franklin, in the preface to his pamphlet, entitled "Considerations on the Nature and Extent of the Authority of the British Parliament," 'many will perhaps be surprised to see the legislative authority of the British Parliament over the Colonies *denied in every instance*. . . . He entered upon them with a view and expectation of being able to trace some constitutional line between those cases in which we ought, and those in which we ought not, to acknowledge the power of Parliament over us. In the prosecution of his inquiries he became fully convinced that *such a line doth not exist;* and that there can be no medium between acknowledging and denying that power in ALL CASES.' . . .

"The following is a Resolution of the Original American Congress on the same subject: 'That the foundation of English liberty, and of all free government, is a right in the people to participate in their Legislative Council; *and as the English Colonists are not represented, and from their local and other circumstances cannot properly be represented, in the British Parliament,* they are entitled to a free and exclusive power of legislation in their several Provincial Legislatures, where their right of representation can alone be preserved in all cases of taxation and internal polity.' . . .

"The famous Jeremy Bentham, in his pamphlet entitled, 'Emancipate your Colonies,' addressed to the National Assembly of France, characterizes the scheme of Parliamentary Representation for the Colonies in the following language: '*Oh, but they will send deputies: and those deputies will govern us as much as we govern them.*'

Illusion! What is that but doubling the mischief instead of lessening it? To give yourself a pretence for governing a million or two of strangers, you admit half a dozen. To govern a million or two of people you don't care about, you admit half a dozen people that don't care about you. To govern a set of people whose business you know nothing about, you encumber yourselves with half a dozen starers, who know nothing about yours. Is this fraternity? Is this liberty and equality? . . . Nay, it is evident and indisputable that it was on this principle of freedom and independence, as far at least as their own internal government was concerned, that the British Colonies in America were originally formed; for, considering the important national interests at stake in the matter, it is not less humiliating than it is melancholy to reflect, that, in the theory and practice of colonization, we have actually been retrograding or going back as a people for the last two hundred and fifty years! 'The fundamental idea,' observes Mr. Merivale, 'of the old or British Colonial policy appears to have been, that wherever a man went, he carried with him the rights of an Englishman, whatever these were supposed to be. . . . This is remarkably proved by the fact, that representative government was seldom expressly granted in the early charters; it was assumed by the Colonists as a matter of right.' . . .

"There are still, indeed, individuals, both in our own and in other Mother Countries of Europe, who cling to the old fallacy of Empire, and regard either the actual or the possible loss of dominion over distant Colonies as an event in the highest degree to be deprecated and deplored. And it is singular enough that one should have to include among such persons—the adherents of an exploded system—so eminent a writer as Mr. Carlyle."

As to the British right of property, and right to the future fruits of it, and to return for outlays in blood, enterprise, and money, we are coolly told:—

"But Great Britain has received an ample compensation for her outlay in planting the Australian Colonies, in another and much more valuable form—in the magnificent outlet she has thereby established for her redundant population; in the valuable and indefinitely extending market for her manufactured goods of all kinds which she has thus created, and in the boundless field she has opened up for the production of the raw material required for her manufactures, and for the employment of her home population. Assuredly, Great Britain has never expended any money for which she will receive an ampler return than she has already received, and will still continue to receive, for all time coming, from the expenditure she incurred in the establishment of the Australian Colonies. Independently of the market for goods of all kinds which these Colonies afford to the Mother Country, to an extent unequalled in any other country of the same population in the world, Great Britain actually received from the Colony of New South Wales alone, during the first ten years, from the introduction of the system of selling the waste lands of the Colony, and devoting a large portion of the proceeds for the promotion of emigration, not less than a million sterling : the whole of which was expended in relieving the Mother Country of a serious public burden by paying for the conveyance of persons of the humbler classes from Great Britain and Ireland to New South Wales."

A pretty relief, to take away our best stuff, if they are to be " relieved " from allegiance and their labour no longer to increase the capital and productive powers, nor the strength, of the Empire ! He again harps thus discordantly : —

" But even, although Great Britain had never received any pecuniary or other compensation for the expenditure she incurred in the establishment of the Australian Colonies, this would in no way have affected the right of these Colonies to their entire freedom and independence, on the attainment of their political majority. The slave has an *absolute* right to his freedom, whether his master has cleared his purchase-money by him or not. The son, who has completed the twenty-first year of his age, has an *absolute* right to entire freedom from parental control, whatever his father may have expended on his board and education. It is the law of nature and the ordinance of God, that the parent should provide for the child during his nonage, without entering him in his ledger as a debtor for the expense of his up-bringing. If the parent has discharged his duty in the case, the child will delight to repay the obligation in whatever way he can. *He will honour his father and mother,* from the instinctive feeling of filial affection, as well as *that his days may be long in the land which the Lord his God shall give him ;* and so far from this feeling being extinguished by the mere fact of his being legally free from all parental control, it will still grow with his growth and strengthen with his strength, till, in the course of nature, he is called to deposit the remains of his venerated parent with sorrow in the grave."

We are informed that a high authority declares this—viz. :

" The advantage is, that the possession of this immense Empire by

England causes the mere name of England to be a real and mighty Power—the greatest Power that now exists in the world."

But it is assumed that this is not merely beside the mark, but vanity ; whereas it is sober and important truth that equally concerns the Colonists.

"Whether the latter are to surrender their natural and inherent rights, merely to gratify the vanity, or to minister to the self-importance of those who are at the centre of the system, is a question which, I conceive, admits but of one answer. It so completely sets aside the golden rule of doing to others as we should wish to be done by, that one can scarcely help feeling ashamed at hearing of such a proposition from any person calling himself an Englishman. Is it either just or right—for that is the question—that the best and dearest interests of any people should be compromised and sacrificed; that their social progress should be impeded and retarded in an endless variety of ways; that they should be refused their proper position among the nations, and degraded to a condition of pitiable and humiliating subserviency— in order to minister to the gratification of this mean, contemptible vanity on the part of another people at the ends of the earth ? For what, I ask, are the British people better than we—the British Colonists of Australia—except that they are twenty to one of us ? But does this give them any right, by the law of nature or the ordinance of God, to govern us ? . . .

"Again, to talk of England keeping the peace of the world, while she has eight hundred millions of debt of her own, incurred almost exclusively through her generally unjust and unnecessary wars, is amusing enough, but it can surely be no reason why British Colonists, who have a natural and inherent right to nationality, should be forced to continue in the very subordinate and unsatisfactory condition of mere dependents and vassals. " *If thou mayest be made free,*" says the apostle Paul (and the advice applies to communities as well as to individuals), "*use it rather.*

" . . Mr. Wakefield's *prestige* is merely another name for *shadow :* it has no substance in it, no real value. And although Earl Grey, in his elaborate but unsuccessful apology for his own mal-administration of the Colonies, ostentatiously expresses his opinion that 'the British Colonial Empire ought to be maintained, because much of the power and influence of Great Britain depends upon her having large Colonial Possessions in different parts of the world ;' as if that were anything to *us*. The question is simply—What solid advantages does

England really derive from her possession of such Dependencies as the Australian Colonies? In answer to this question, the late Sir George Lewis, in his able and singularly honest work, on 'The Government of Dependencies,' enumerates the advantages which a Parent State or dominant country derives from its supremacy over a Dependency as follows:—

" . . . 2. *Assistance for military or naval purposes.*—Such assistance was very frequently rendered by the earlier Colonists of America, in the wars of the Mother Country with France, which had then an extensive Empire in that country; but no such assistance could either be expected or would be necessary now. It is worthy of remark that the celebrated Dr. Adam Smith considered the contribution of revenue and military force as so essential to the very idea of a Colony, that he regarded any Dependency as utterly valueless that did not contribute either the one or the other. His words are as follows:—

" 'Countries which contribute neither revenue nor military force towards the support of the Empire cannot be considered as provinces. They may, perhaps, be considered as appendages, as a sort of splendid and showy equipage of the Empire.'

" 3. *Advantages to the dominant country from its trade with the Dependency.*—Since the commencement of the present Free Trade system, no special advantage can be derived by the Mother Country from this source."

Is this true? May she not at least stipulate that she shall be laid under no special *disadvantage*? She might without effrontery.

" 4. *Facilities afforded by Dependencies to the dominant country for the emigration of its surplus population, and for an advantageous employment of its capital.*—Sir George Lewis admits, however, that in order to secure this advantage to the Mother Country, it is not necessary that the Colony should be a Dependency of the Parent State.

" Sir George Lewis also enumerates the advantages derivable by a Dependency from its dependence on the dominant country, under the following heads, viz. :—

" 1. *Protection by the dominant country.* . .
" 2. *Pecuniary assistance by the dominant country.* . .
" 3. *Commercial advantages* . . .

" There is therefore not one substantial advantage derivable, either by the Mother Country on the one hand, or by the Australian Colonies on the other, from the continuance of the present connexion of domination and dependency. The only advantage remaining to the Mother Country is a merely imaginary one—the glory of the thing."

Surely, surely, this is exaggeration and obscuration. The question, however, is not mainly one of hard cold calculable "advantage."

See how the Doctor himself writes about what Colonies take compared with ex-Colonies :—

"When it is considered that every inhabitant of the United States consumes only about seven shillings and sixpence worth of British produce and manufactures annually, whereas every inhabitant of the Australian Colonies consumes from seven to ten pounds worth—[population of New South Wales in 1869 = 485,358; imports, £3,514,285, or £7 7s. per head]—the loss which **Great Britain** sustains in this way must be immense."

The following is noteworthy, not because of the dangerous mistake of Sir H. Parnell, but for the exhibition it gives of the vast sums the United Kingdom has spent on Colonies which yet the Australian preacher from the golden rule would snatch away without compensation, using such language as we have seen.

"'With respect to Canada (including our other Possessions on the Continent of North America),' observes the late Sir Henry Parnell, 'no case can be made out to show that we should not have *every commercial advantage* we are supposed now to have, if it were made *an independent State*. Neither our manufactures, foreign commerce, nor shipping, would be injured by such a measure. On the other hand, what has the nation lost by Canada? Fifty or sixty millions have already been expended.'"

I do doubt the following very, very much :—

"No one now really doubts that the separation of our North American Colonies has been, in an economical sense, advantageous to us. And yet precisely the same arguments are current at this very day respecting the superior profit of **Colonial** commerce, and the wealth arising from Colonial domination, which were in every one's mouth before that great event had occurred, and by its results confounded all such calculations. So easily does our reason contrive to forget the strongest lessons, or to evade their force, when prejudice and love of power warp it in the contrary direction. . . .

"The independence of the American Colonies furnishes an apt illustration; for although the Continental nations believed that this change had struck a deadly blow at England, they soon forgot their false theory when they observed the inexhaustible resources which she displayed during the French war."

Not resources in sons of her own be it remembered and pondered.

Let us, *per contra*, think how mighty a Confederation would have existed if the whole English-speaking people had been always and until now happily united. There is yet a "next best" open.

"The grand question of the day in England is that of Emigration: and considering that the population of the United Kingdom is increasing at the rate of a quarter of a million per annum, while the difficulty of obtaining employment and comfortable subsistence for the industrious classes is also constantly increasing, it is no matter of wonder that that question should be one of intense interest to every lover of his country. How, then, it will be asked, will Australia respond to the desires and necessities of the Mother Country, whether as a series of separate Colonies, as at present, or as a sovereign and independent State? These two questions I shall endeavour to answer consecutively."

"So early as the year 1835, when the Colony of New South Wales extended from Cape Capricorn to Bass's Straits, and the fund arising from the sale of its waste lands on the Wakefield principle—that is, appropriating the proceeds for the promotion of emigration—was becoming considerable, I published a series of papers in Sydney, pointing out the paramount importance of that fund for insuring the welfare and advancement of the Colony, through the progressive introduction into its territory of numerous industrious and virtuous families and individuals from the Mother Country. In these papers I laid down and advocated the two following principles, viz.:—1st. That the waste lands of Australia were not the property of the actual Colonists, but of all the inhabitants of the British Empire; and 2nd. That the best mode of expending the funds accruing from the sale of these lands was in the promotion of the emigration of industrious and virtuous families and individuals from the Mother Country to Australia, in numbers proportioned to the population of each of the three kingdoms respectively." . . .

Would the loss described, not too strongly, in the following have been avoided, or will there be avoidance in future, as the effect of severance? I fear not.

"And the result is precisely what might have been anticipated—colonization directs itself towards the waste lands of the United States, while those of the British Colonies, with a much better climate, are passed by and disregarded. Witness the emigration from the United Kingdom during the years 1852 and 1853: it amounted

In 1852, to 368,764.
In 1853, to 318,680.

And whither did these emigrants direct their steps? Why, not fewer than 224,000 in 1852, and 225,258 in 1853, emigrated from Great Britain and Ireland to the United States; while the emigration to British America, during the same years, respectively, was in 1852, only 33,563; and in 1853, only 30,563; and to Australia, in 1852, 87,000; and in 1853, 59,931. Notwithstanding, therefore, the powerful impulse that was given to emigration throughout the United Kingdom, by the discovery of gold in Australia, the full tide of emigration from Great Britain was still directed towards the United States, and the claims of the British Colonies, with all their superior advantages, were treated with derision. In one word, this humiliating state of things was entirely the result of bad government and the lust of empire on the part of Great Britain."

Here is one reason why regard for the welfare of the Colonies should lead even separatists to hesitate and pause:—

"There is a regular Anti-Immigration League in existence in Victoria, and there is a considerable number of persons of the same opinion in New South Wales. But I am happy to state that there is a large majority of the people of the latter Colony strongly in favour of an extensive immigration from the Mother Country, and strongly disposed to make the requisite sacrifice, in the way of a *bonus* in land, for the accomplishment of so important an object."

The Doctor is sound on this point:—

"I hold it to be one of the urgent necessities of the times that a *bonus* in land should be held forth to all who can pay their own passage to Australia."

Now, where would the lands be, or at whose disposal, if the Colonies go? Happily, all has not yet been *given* away. See *Parliamentary Returns*, 1870.

What we now reproduce is "an owre true tale":—

"A Draft Constitution had been drawn up by the Legislative Council of New South Wales, in the year 1853, which was approved of and enacted by the Imperial Parliament in 1855; the Colony granting Her Majesty a Civil List, and Her Majesty conceding, in lieu of it, to the Colonial Legislature all the *Droits* of the Crown, and in particular all the waste lands of the territory in absolute and perpetual possession. Now I have no hesitation in stating—as one of the representatives of the people in the Legislature of New South Wales, for upwards of a quarter of a century—that, if the rights and interests of Great Britain, as a great colonizing Power, had been taken into consideration, on that most important occasion, by the Secretary of State for the Colonies, a very different arrangement, and one of transcendant importance to the Mother Country, might have been effected with perfect facility. The importance of immigration, both to the Mother Country and to the Australian Colonies, had then been so long and so extensively acknowledged, that if the Secretary of State, whose bounden duty it was to have duly considered the rights and interests of both parties in the case, had merely insisted on attaching to the Imperial Act a proviso to the effect that one-half of the funds accruing from the sales of all waste lands in Australia should be appropriated, for a certain period at least, to the promotion of emigration from the United Kingdom, the arrangement would have been cordially acceded to by the Australian public. . . . At the general election in New South Wales, in 1851, several of the candidates put forth the idea that, as the discovery of gold would send out plenty of emigrants to the Colony, no part of the land fund ought in future to be appropriated for immigration purposes, but that the whole of it should be applied for the construction of roads and bridges, &c. But Great Britain has a deep interest in preventing any such measure from being carried—she has a deep interest, on behalf of her industrious and virtuous poor, in insisting upon the continuance of the present arrangement for the appropriation of at least one-half of the land fund for the promotion of emigration from the United Kingdom." . . .

"'I am, therefore, decidedly of opinion that Great Britain should on no account surrender the absolute control of the waste lands to any mere Provincial Legislature, and that she should make it a *sine quâ non*, in a Treaty of Independence with the General or National Government, that one-half of the proceeds of the sales of all waste lands throughout the Union should be appropriated as at present for the promotion of emigration from Great Britain and Ireland."

"'This arrangement would effectually insure a thoroughly British population for the Australian provinces; which, I confess—with the best possible feelings towards foreigners of all nations—I regard as a matter of essential importance for their welfare and advancement. Under such an arrangement, also, the National Government of the Australian Union would virtually be a mere *agency*, and as far as the Mother Country is concerned, an *unpaid agency*, for carrying out the first grand object of colonization for Great Britain—viz., the providing of an eligible outlet for her redundant population. The Australian provinces would, therefore, although formally free and independent, be in reality a series of *Tributary States* to Great Britain; paying her a large amount of *tribute* for the promotion of emigration from her shores every year: for although the benefit would be mutual and equal, the arrangement would necessarily take the form of a large annual contribution to the British treasury from Australia—probably not less in amount than £150,000 (a hundred and fifty thousand) a-year.'

" By Clause II. of the Imperial Act 18 and 19 Vict., cap. 54, passed 16th July, 1855, it is enacted that—' The entire management and control of the waste lands belonging to the Crown in the said Colony, and also the appropriation of the gross proceeds of the sales of any such lands, and of all other proceeds and revenues of the same, from whatever source arising within the said Colony, including all royalties, mines, and minerals, shall be vested in the Legislature of the said Colony.'

" And it is also enacted by Clause L of the same Act, as follows:—' The said several sums mentioned in Schedules A, B, and C shall be accepted and taken by Her Majesty, her heirs and successors, by way of Civil List, instead of all territorial, casual, and other revenues of the Crown (including all royalties), from whatever source, arising within the said Colony, and to the disposal of which the Crown may be entitled either absolutely or conditionally, or otherwise howsoever.'

" The three Schedules above referred to are as follows:—

" *Schedule A.*
" Salaries of public offices £20,550
" *Schedule B.*
" Pensions chargeable £13,950
" *Schedule C* (now in process of extinction).
" Public worship............................ £28,000

" This famous Act was passed on the 16th July, 1855—Lord John Russell being then Secretary of State for the Colonies. The following

Paper, for which I am indebted to the courtesy of George F. Wise, Esq., Agent for Immigration in New South Wales, being an abstract of his yearly reports for three different periods—will show the reader how immensely valuable to Great Britain, as a field for emigration, was the magnificent estate which was thus virtually thrown away."

Dr. Lang quotes fairly Mr. Froude:—

" 'The Colonies,' says an able writer, 'contain virgin soil sufficient to employ and feed five times as many people as are now crowded into Great Britain and Ireland. Nothing is needed but arms to cultivate it; while here, among ourselves, are millions of able-bodied men unwillingly idle, clamouring for work, with their families starving on their hands. What more simple than to bring the people and the land together! . . . . The land, we are told impatiently, is no longer now ours. A few years ago it *was* ours, but to save the Colonial Office trouble, we made it over to the local government, and now we have no more right over it than we have over the prairies of Texas. If it were so, *the more shame to the politicians who let drop so precious an inheritance.*'"

It may be worth while to produce some of the considerations by which the Doctor would coax the Australians to adopt his views. They need not defend their trade nor their coasts. They will profit by the ex-Mother Country's and other European misfortunes. It will be noticed, he would not be downright mean.

"Neither is it the interest of Great Britain that the carrying trade with Australia should pass into the hands of the Australian people; and so long as she enjoys her present monopoly, it will be her own direct interest to protect that trade, as she is well able and can well afford to do. . . . Nay, removed as she is from the field of European strife so much farther than America, Australia would be still less likely to suffer in any way from European warfare. Her flag would be respected by all the belligerents; and the prevalence of a general European war, during which the flags of these belligerents would be in constant danger from each other, would only have the effect of raising Australia, as the long French War did the United States, in circumstances precisely similar, into a first-rate Maritime Power. In such an event, many even of the lovers of peace in the old world would gladly emigrate to her territory, to enrol themselves among her free people, and thereby to avail themselves of such protection as her flag would afford them, both by sea and land, when Europe had been again transformed into a field of blood. But even on the supposition that there should be no Australian marine, in the event of a general European war, if Great Britain were no longer able to protect the Australian trade in her own merchant ships, from French or Russian cruisers, our elder brother Jonathan would gladly step in to relieve her of her present monopoly, and to frank our commerce with her Stars and Stripes to all the world."

" England would thenceforth be relieved of the enormous cost of protecting the Australian Colonies in time of war, while their profitable trade would continue to flow in the old channels, and be rapidly and indefinitely increased."

"'Oh! but that is the very case in point,' I shall be told. 'Great Britain would defend and protect us in case of war, as she would be bound to do. She would have frigates cruising off Cape Leeuwin; she would have others off both Capes of New Zealand, and others still off this stormy Cape Horn, where you are now writing, and scarce able to guide the pen from the rolling and plunging of the ship in this tempestuous sea. Besides, she would have ships of war cruising along our whole line of coast, and occasionally enlivening us with their presence in our harbours; and, what is best of all, *she would make her own people pay all the expenses, without asking a farthing from us!*' Now this is a great deal too much for Great Britain to do for us. We have no desire whatever to put her to the slightest trouble or expense in the matter, or to tax her people a single farthing for our protection and defence—simply because it is quite unnecessary."

But he foresees difficulties. The British people at home must see that all is right before they allow the Colonist to let go the painter.

" Under the present Colonial system there are always petty jealousies subsisting between the different Colonies, even of the same group; which, if they were all sovereign and independent, might prove a source of repulsion rather than of attraction."

" I repeat it, it is not for the interest either of Great Britain, or of the world at large, to permit the formation of a number of petty sovereignties in this hemisphere; and so long as it is in the power of the Mother Country to bind together the whole of the eastern provinces into one great nation—one mighty Power of the future in the Pacific—that will condescend to play 'no second fiddle' to Brother Jonathan, but will claim perfect equality with him from the first—

her proper course in the matter is plain and obvious, and cannot be mistaken."

He hopes half of Australia will be big enough for a "nation."

"As separate and independent communities, the present Australian Colonies would be comparatively insignificant, and would have no weight or influence in the family of nations; but seven such provinces combined, with the whole eastern coast-line towards the Pacific as the measure of their Empire, would at once form the first Power in the Southern Hemisphere."

But, alas! the more important of the seven would not "bite." (See his Preface.)

He has no good word to say in behalf of the London Colonists who remonstrated against such heresies as his and against a certain policy (if policy it is) that elsewhere is cherished.

"Nay, these pseudo-patriots have summoned both Earl Grey and his Grace the Duke of Manchester to the rescue, to prevent, if possible, the awful consummation they anticipate. Earl Grey, in a letter to one of the patriots, Mr. A. Youl, of date, Howick, Bilton, Northumberland, September 4th, 1869, solemnly declares that '*the breaking up of the great Colonial Empire of England would, in my opinion, be a calamity to the Colonies, to this country, and to the world.*' The Duke of Manchester also, in a letter which was read at the annual meeting of the Social Science Congress, in [October] last, addressed to Sir Stafford Northcote, M.P., President, expresses himself as follows:—'*If we lose our Colonies, our power is gone.* On the other hand, if we amalgamate our Colonies with us, if we take them into partnership with us in the government of the Empire, I am convinced we should greatly increase our power. It seems to me that the only practical plan would be to substitute for the Colonial Office a Council, containing representatives of the United Kingdom and the Colonies in fair proportion according to their wealth and the number of their inhabitants.'

"Now (without reverting to the subject of Parliamentary Representation for the Colonies, which the Duke of Manchester seems to desiderate) it is particularly worthy of remark that precisely the same fears that are now entertained, and the same dismal forebodings that are now put forth by Earl Grey and the Duke, in regard to the probable result of the separation of any of our present Colonies from the Mother Country, were entertained and put forth a century ago."

IGNORES IDEA OF IMPERIAL FEDERATION. 85

The most marvellous thing in the whole book is, that in only one passage is a Council of the Empire, or an Imperial Confederation, mentioned; that passage is the foregoing, where it is introduced by a sort of accident; when mentioned it is misunderstood and receives the go-by. I am sorry to say that the answers given to Lord Sandon's allusion to this, the alone promising, solution of the Colonial difficulty, during last Session of Parliament, were equally devoid of reasoning,—equally showed that its value and acceptability were unappreciated or misapprehended.

Our enthusiastic Colonist wrote this book because " there is no subject on which the literature of Great Britain presents so complete a blank" as the principles of Colonization. He aspires [to fill the blank. I wish he had done it better.

Perhaps I do a greater service to the literature of the subject when I republish from " Hansard" the following short passage from the speech of the Member for Liverpool :—

". . . Who, then, wanted to part with the Colonies? Did the working classes? Could anybody mistake the meaning of those meetings which had been held within the last few months on the subject? The depth of feeling among the artizans on this subject was not yet fully appreciated by the country. Was it not manifest that our working classes looked upon the Colonies as their land of promise, and regarded those distant territories as the birthright, so to speak, of their sons and daughters? . . . He could scarcely imagine how any sect of men could desire to see our great Confederation broken up at such a moment as the present. The general tendency of men at the present day was in quite the opposite direction. The tendency of the day was in favour of large nationalities, and the day of small nations was past. Could we shut our eyes to the fact that nationalities were everywhere endeavouring to group themselves into large States? Germany was forgetting her divisions, and grouping herself into one powerful State; Italy had happily almost accomplished the same work; and the races in the North were following out the same process. Why should we, at such a moment, in obedience to the opinions of any set of men, however enlightened, crumble up that great Empire which Providence had placed in our hands? It was surely our duty to take the opposite course, and carry out the work we were called upon, as a first-class nation, to fulfil. Could it be imagined that we should long remain a first-class Power if Colony after Colony were stripped from us? Could we, under such circumstances, long retain our grasp on India? We owed it as a duty to our own people not to shrink, from any feeling of laziness, from maintaining the proud position which we had acquired, and to keep open these outlets for our teeming populations; while we owed it also to the people of those new Continents, to whom it was a great advantage to have the admixture of our old civilization and to start with our great traditions, not to break that tie which attracted to them the cultivated classes of this country, but which would cease to exist if they did not continue to be subjects of the same Crown. The question was a great and a large one; and it had, he thought, been very well put in a despatch lately sent to the Government by that distinguished man, Sir Philip Wodehouse, who spoke of responsible government in the Colonies as meaning in the end independence, and therefore separation from the Mother Country. He believed Sir Philip Wodehouse was wrong; but, nevertheless, his deliberate expressions showed what opinions were afloat, and convinced him that the question of the relations between ourselves and the Colonies must be faced as a whole, and handled in a broad and comprehensive spirit. Now, that was the point which he would entreat the House to consider very carefully, whether we were to look forward calmly and contentedly to the future sketched out in that despatch, or to use our best exertions to consolidate those semi-independent communities into one great Empire with ourselves. It was, no doubt, the harder, but it was the more glorious task: it was, no doubt, a difficult problem, and would require the exercise of all the statesmanship which this country possessed for its solution; but he hoped that no luxurious laziness, no timidity, no shrinking from labour would induce that House to decline the noble work of reconstructing, and so far as things on earth could be so, of rendering everlasting our British Empire."

EMIGRATION.

The Thirtieth General Report of the Emigration Commissioners is a most interesting and informing document or volume. It is obtainable from the Queen's Printers for a shilling. The following are clippings:—

"In 1869 less than three-fourths were British subjects, the remainder being foreigners who merely pass through this country on their way to North America. The following table shows the number and nationality of the emigrants who have left the United Kingdom during the last seven years:—

Year.	English.	Scotch.	Irish.	Foreigners.	Not distinguished.	Total.
1863	61,243	15,230	116,391	7,833	23,061	223,758
1864	56,618	15,035	115,428	16,942	4,877	208,900
1865	61,345	12,870	100,676	28,619	6,291	209,801
1866	58,856	12,307	98,890	26,691	8,138	204,882
1867	55,494	12,866	88,622	31,193	7,778	195,953
1868	58,268	14,954	64,965	51,956	6,182	196,325
1869	90,416	22,559	73,325	65,752	5,975	258,027

"In the emigration of last year the most noticeable fact is the large increase in the number of English and Scotch emigrants. For the first time since we have any trustworthy returns the number of English emigrants exceeded the Irish. With the exception of 1854, the number was the largest that ever left the United Kingdom in a single year. There was, however, this difference between the English emigrants of 1854 and of last year, that in 1854 of 90,966 emigrants, 47,132, or neary 52 per cent., went to Australia, while last year of 90,416 emigrants 77,710, or nearly 86 per cent., went to North America. In the former case they were attracted by the hope of gain; in the latter they were driven forth by the fear of distress.

"The emigration of 1869 was thus distributed:—

To the United States	203,001
„ British North America	33,891
„ Australia and New Zealand	14,901
„ all other places	6,234
	258,026

"Of the emigration to the United States:—

The English	formed	31·06 per cent.
The Irish	,,	32·75 ,,
Foreigners	,,	25·29 ,,
Scotch	,,	8·48 ,,
Not distinguished	,,	2·42 ,,
		100 ,,

"Of the whole number who emigrated to North America in 1869, amounting to 236,892, no less than 225,685, or 95·27 per cent., went in steamers, and only 11,207, or 4·73 per cent., went in sailing vessels. The resort to steamers in the emigration to America has been uninterruptedly progressive. In 1863 it amounted to only 45·85 per cent. of the whole number. In 1867 it had increased to 92·86 per cent., in 1868 to 93·16 per cent., and last year to 95·27 per cent. It is scarcely possible to exaggerate the advantage which emigrants obtain by passages in steamers, both in the shortness of the voyage and the better accommodation. The cost of passage is, however, from 30 to 50 per cent. higher than in sailing ships, showing that the emigrants are, at least, not in circumstances which compel them to subject all other considerations to cheapness.

"The mortality on the voyage, as far as we have returns, was very small, the number of deaths in steamers, among 211,879 emigrants, having been only 119, or ·05 per cent. Assuming the voyage at fourteen days, this would be equal to a mortality of 14 per 1,000 per annum."

"Emigration from this country, as has been pointed out, first assumed gigantic proportions in 1847, on the occurence of the famine in Ireland. Between 1847 and 1869 inclusive, there sailed from the United Kingdom 5,084,571 souls, of whom there went—

To the United States	3,496,549
,, British North America	610,343
,, Australia	847,016
,, all other parts	130,663
	5,084,571

"For the present purpose the emigration to the Australian Colonies and other places, which cannot be regarded as relief Emigration, may be put aside, and the emigration to the United States and British North America be alone considered.

"The number of emigrants to North America between 1847 and 1869 was 4,106.892; deducting—

Cabin passengers...............	259,141	
Foreigners	338,213	597,354
There remain		3,509,538—

equal to about 3,112,144 statute adults, who may be considered to have been British-born subjects of the labouring class. The passages of these emigrants can scarcely have cost less than 15,000.000*l.*, or, on an average, upwards of 650,000*l.* a-year. The whole of this sum has been provided out of private resources, in great measure out of the remittances from the United States and Canada made by previous emigrants."

"In South Australia the funds set apart by law for emigration, which, in June, 1868, amounted to 360,000*l.*, and cannot now be less than half a million, have, in great measure, been appropriated to another service, and Bills have been three times passed by the Assembly, but rejected by the Council, to make that appropriation final."

"From a variety of causes the great bulk of the immigrants who arrived in the Dominion have only passed through to the United States, conferring no advantage, but the contrary, on the Dominion. During the last four years the number who arrived and who remained have been :—

	Arrived.	Remained.
1866	51,795	10,091
1867	57,878	10,066
1868	71,448	12,765
1869	75,800	18,630

"NEW SOUTH WALES.

"The land revenue of New South Wales during the year 1869 was :—

Land sales...	£275,726	12	7
Balances of conditional purchases	19,525	16	6
Interest on land sales to conditional purchasers......	24,360	8	7
Rent of land, first-class settled districts	22,424	12	1
Rent of runs, second-class settled and unsettled districts...	213,326	1	11
Assessment on runs, second-class settled and unsettled districts.....................................	9,522	19	11
Fees on transfer of runs	896	0	0
Quit rents...	69	13	4

	£	s.	d.
Licences to cut timber, &c., on Crown lands	1,790	12	3
Mineral leases	5,412	2	0
Leases of auriferous lands	4,634	16	8
Miners' rights	5,243	5	0
Business licences	655	0	0
Survey of land	118	18	1
Miscellaneous	326	12	9
	£584,033	11	8

["Our lands," therefore, go to lighten, by more than a pound a-head, the annual taxation of our friends who have jilted us in the matter of liability for the national debt!]

"This was an increase, as compared with 1868, of 42,804*l.* 8s. 7d.

"The gold revenue during the year was—

	£	s.	d.
Duty on gold	16,840	19	7
Fees for export and conveyance of gold, &c.	8,152	6	10
	£24,993	6	5

being an increase, as compared with 1868, of 234*l.* 7s. 3d.

"The total revenue proper in 1868 and 1869 was—

	£	s.	d.
1868	2,405,356	15	2
1869	2,202,970	5	10

showing an increase of 157,613*l.* 10s. 8d.

"The total expenditure in 1869 was 2,617,205*l.* 3s. 10d."

"QUEENSLAND.

"The land sales in Queensland in 1868, the latest date for which we have returns, were—

	Extent.			Amount realized.		
	A.	R.	P.	£	s.	d.
By public auction	52,235	3	9	57,080	5	3
By pre-emptive purchases	1,600	0	0	1,674	10	0
Mineral sections	3,120	0	0	2,182	10	0
Improved allotments	114	0	38	148	7	3
	57,070	0	7	61,085	12	6
Leased under Act 30 Vict., No. 12	3,436	2	28	431	14	11
	60,506	2	35	61,517	7	5

[So the Queensland folks get only about 12s. per head off their annual taxation by disposing of land—which is "capital," not proper income.]

I am favoured by the Secretary of the Emigration Board with the following figures, which show that the first nine months of 1870 have been very active in the Emigration business. Remembering that a large proportion of emigrants to Canada have their destination in the United States, the reader will see that the Colonies, especially those in Africa and Australia, are still neglected. The number of English and Scotch is striking. Considering their destination, it is appalling in the eyes of every man who realizes the loss their removal causes to the Empire:—

RETURN of EMIGRATION from Ports in the United Kingdom, at which there are Emigration Officers, for the period from the 1st January to 30th September, 1870.

Destination.	English.	Scotch.	Irish.	Foreigners.	Not Distinguished.	Total.
United States............	56,326	13,942	60,755	31,866	2,954	165,843
N. American Colonies.	18,316	3,270	2,098	7,699	55	31,438
Australian Colonies ...	8,532	1,720	2,350	275	3	12,880
All other Places.........	1,264	235	149	200	839	2,687
Total	84,438	19,167	65,352	40,040	3,851	212,848

Government Emigration Board,   S. WALCOTT.
8, Park Street, Westminster,
December 15, 1870.

It may be useful to consider what is the *value* of the transference which the United Kingdom has allowed to be made by Emigration. This can be exhibited only by a *money* estimate—a coarse, though true, method of reckoning, which may be accepted for the purpose. If we fix the sum at £500 for each adult male, £100 for each adult female, £50 for each child, and £10 for each infant—figures which, considering the class and character of the emigrants, are fair enough—we find that the United Kingdom parted last year with a productive and "tending" power worth no less than *fifty-four millions sterling*.

Of the above, I regret to say, *forty-eight millions* may be assumed to be no longer British, but now foreign.

The contribution to which—if we may conceive that there were an equal rate laid in the United Kingdom for the extinction of the National Debt—each average emigrant would be liable appears to be a sum of between £35 and £50. So that last year the population which remained became subject, by means of emigration, to an enhanced burden or liability represented by a capital sum that may be estimated at between *nine* and *thirteen millions sterling*. That is, the emigrants shirked and shifted upon us their obligation to pay taxes for interest to the extent of half-a-million a-year.

I have given no estimate of the *loss* inflicted on the nation by immigration from the Empire, of *consuming power*, nor of *power of creating*, for neighbour tradesmen, *the means of earning their livelihood*. The public mind too generally is directed only to the consumption of great *manufactures* and of *imports*. I desiderate information, from such accomplished statists as Dr. Levi or Mr. Dudley Baxter, as to the annual *profit* or free income which British *tradesmen* and people who are employed at jobbing work and repairs, in serving, &c., are deprived of by the expatriation of an average emigrant. Let me set it down—and it is a mere guess—at no more than the very safe figure of 10*l.* (including in this a quota of rent), and the total national loss in this item alone amounts up to nigh *two millions* sterling a-year; or, say, what would maintain in comparative comfort 100,000 persons within the Queen's dominions, instead of a like number of persons in foreign countries. In this reckoning no allowance is made for the profit or employment which these 100,000 persons in their turn produce.

The world has got so used to British blindness, or softness, or goodness, that it reckons on our support, and assumes that a service is done us, when propositions are made to "relieve us of" and draw away to foreign parts our best population. Just last summer I was present at a meeting of one of our greatest philanthropic, so-called "National Associations," called to welcome an American gentleman whose object or purpose seemed to be to lay before us what the United States could and would do in that way, the Association's favour being most implicitly relied on.

PROCEEDINGS OF THE ROYAL COLONIAL INSTITUTE, 1869.

DECEMBER 22.—I have to-day received the First Report of the Institute, and now present some clippings from a valuable Paper contributed by my highly esteemed friend, Mr. Westgarth, late Member of the Legislative Council of Victoria, and well known as an author of works on Australia :—

" The great aim of the Colonies has been their own self-government: nor were they unsuccessful in their aim, even from the first; for although the Imperial response on this point of Colonial policy had been in the earlier times of a very negative character, yet neglect was generally the happier fate in days when the public sentiment at home was anything but sympathetic with the views and wishes of Colonies. Latterly the response has been altogether different, and the relations increasingly cordial. . . .

" But during the reign of George III., the great development which circumstances gave to the power of the Crown, and to autocratic sentiment in the relations of government, led to those well-known high-handed proceedings as to Colonies which resulted so disastrously at the time, but have led to so useful a lesson since. 'The Colonies,' it had been then said, 'had no right to manufacture for themselves even a nail or a horse-shoe;' and subsequently when, in a like spirit, taxes were attempted to be levied for the home exchequer, the cup of endurance ran over. Ireland and Shetland, it was argued, contributed to the Imperial treasury, and why not the American part of the Empire ? The theory might be right, but all else was wrong. . . .

" Each Colony had its ' British party,' which, ignoring or despising the great body of the Colonists, put itself forward to the Home Government as the only reliable loyal link of the community. Mr. Gladstone might have added that there was still another party that in those days characterized each Colony—a party more or less strong, more or less weak, but always in being—the party that advocated separation from, and independence of, the Mother Country. Both these parties have since alike disappeared under the late successive steps of cordial approach between the Parent State and the Colonial offspring. I am bound to add, as a Colonist who was a witness of the case, that these steps have been conceded with like cordiality by each of the two great political parties at home; for whether a Conservative or a Liberal has held the Colonial reins, each in turn has been liberal, in the usual sense of the word, to the Colonies.

"Several striking features already stand forth, claiming to comprise our permanent practical principles of Colonial policy and government: 1. None of our Colonies, from the strongest down to the weakest, contributes, or is required to contribute, anything whatever to the Mother Country. 2. The legislation for the Colonies is now practically placed in the hands of their respective local legislatures and government. 3. It may now be affirmed as the Imperial policy, that no Colony will be held to allegiance against its own will. . . .

"I am a Colonist old enough to recollect not only when each Colony had its Separation and Independence party, but when those who took such aims felt that they meant rebellion and war. But now, Colonial loyalty is a thing undoubted, and whatever remains of a separative feeling has cropped out upon the home soil.

"What, then, are the mutual uses and advantages of the Mother Country and her Colonies? . . .

"Take Australasia, for instance, whose total trade, according to the Colonial import and export returns twenty years ago, amounted to eight millions, and is now seventy millions. . . .

"Now we must bear in mind how much trade runs in the groove of the nationality. . . .

"Whatever is to be learned, on the one side or the other, comes alike with more authority and more acceptance under the sentiment of a common citizenship. . . .

"A more important illustration is that connected with free trade principles, now so generally accepted here as the true solution of a long and arduous contest. Some of the Colonies have indeed inclined to 'protection' since assuming self-government, but it has always been with moderation and a sort of apologetic hesitancy, and any secondary degree of successful backsliding, if I may so call it, has been the result of compromise with a vigorous local opposition. . . .

"How often we revel in great schemes of emigration, by which the excess of people here may, to mutual benefit, fill up the wastes of the Colonies. The necessities of the subject ever bring it back to us, and we always hope, spite of all past difficulties, for a system adequate to the wants in both cases. And who shall say that in the general race of modern progress this one question is to stand still, and to remain unsolved? But if we break from our Colonies, we at once throw up this noble national domain, its broad acres, and its virgin soil. We cede its millions of future homes, and lose all that cordial co-operation and guidance which we may ever expect from those our fellow-countrymen already there; and our dreams, our hopes, and our plans are at an end.

"Our age is especially characterized by an onward march of nations, and our English-speaking peoples are at the head of this grand race in all those substantial considerations that make up the idea of "progress." We must not halt, and still less lose ground, in such a busy throng. We are, in fact, so much used to the van of that progress as to feel out of place elsewhere. An honourable and inspiring rivalry pervades the world. The great transatlantic people, because they are our second selves, and planted out under a certain superiority of material circumstances, are already, with characteristic dash, full abreast of their parental nation; and we shall certainly be second in the race if we are severed from the uncramped areas and the fresh impetuous life of our Colonies.

"The British Empire, as it now stands, in point of geographical extent, of population, of power in its many-sided aspects, and of effective world-moving civilization, is the greatest spectacle of its kind in history; and may we not heartily cherish the belief that a fabric so strikingly distinguished, so grand, and so useful, will be long maintained by its component members as one united nationality?"

EXTRACT FROM A PRIVATE LETTER FROM CANADA.

"England seems determined to get clear of us at any cost. It will be easily and soon done. Uncle Sam has only to smile on the next Fenian invasion, which is even now talked of, and we must knock under. What can four millions do against forty? Annexation looms up very strong in the future, and unless a more friendly disposition is shown in England the feeling will grow."

December 9, 1870.

I am favoured with a presentation copy of "The Rising Tide of Irreligion, Pauperism, Immorality, and Death in Glasgow, by the Rev. Jas. Johnston, 1871," and extract the following lines:—

	Population.	Non-churchgoing Protestants.	Paupers.	Criminals.	Deaths.
1868	447,000	130,000	28,061	24,832	13,825
Increase in ten years.	72,000	25,000	5,825	9,100	2,893

This is not the place to speak of the fearfully solemn "burden" which a prophet of old might have been charged with, in relation to the evils set forth in that plain-speaking *brochure*. The figures are adduced to enforce the mischiefs which concentration for trade's sake in large cities generates or involves, and especially the frightful prospect which lies before this nation if manufacturing and commercial prosperity is to proceed, in the future, with the same sad and shameful accompaniments as in the past; or if, in absence of such prosperity, extensive emigration shall skim off the better-disposed parts of the population, and leave behind all the *residuum*.

Hominum generi universo cultura agrorum est salutaris.

A word in conclusion :—

The idea of a possible coming disturbance of the relations between the Mother Country and the Colonies may have a most prejudicial effect in deterring capitalists and emigrants from betaking themselves to and occupying "the Colonial field." It is therefore most desirable that a satisfactory and permanent re-settlement of these relations should be carried out with as much speed as is consistent with the due deliberation which is befitting the novelty and the vast and growing importance of the work.

SIGHS OF A CANADIAN.

The following, from the *Edinburgh Daily Review* of 27th December, is by " A Colonist " :—

" There is a growing belief among us that that party which believes that Colonies are a mere source of expense and weakness to the Mother Country is strong, and is growing stronger. As a taste of this indifference as to Colonies, we see Lord Granville snubbing New Zealand. . . . But we are told, first, that we must provide for our internal peace—nothing could be fairer—and now we are told that we must erect fortifications, arm and drill our Militia, to be prepared to defend our country, at our own expense, against a foreign foe—that if we want a single company of soldiers to man our fortresses we must pay for them, although we shall not command them—and if we want a rifle we must buy it. Nay, the few rifles which were used by our Volunteers in repelling Fenian attempts, not against Canada surely, but against Great Britain, were only lent for the occasion, and the damages, amounting to the paltry sum of about 800*l.*, have been rigorously exacted.

" We do not ask to be treated better than the inhabitants of Manchester or Glasgow would have been, had they been attacked by Fenians, but we think we have a right to expect the same treatment. Had the rich Corporations of either of these cities furnished arms and men, and, in default of military, had repelled the brigands, Parliament would have voted thanks and paid the bill without hesitation. But Canada has done this; our Volunteers took up arms at once, left their employments, exposed their lives, and shed their blood, too, to repel the public enemy; yet our Provincial Government pays all the expense, and is even charged with the price of the rifles damaged in this imperial service. Plainly told, our people are forced to take up arms on account of a question which concerns the whole empire; but because our country was made the scene of operations, we are compelled to pay the piper, and find the pipes to the bargain.

" Absurd as it was and is, the Fenian tries to strike Great Britain over Canada's shoulder; surely, when she beats back the enemy she might expect some better acknowledgment of the service than to be compelled to pay for the weapon which was broken in the fight.

"We do not yet believe that in the event of a war with America England would expect us to pay and arm our Militia from Colonial funds alone; yet the policy which calls upon us at our own expense to arm and fight against the public enemy, and the treatment which we have received in this shabby damaged-rifle matter, would almost warrant us in believing that henceforth we may look to England for allies perhaps, but not for fellow-citizens.

"There is no occasion to continue these arguments; what unsettles the feelings of the most loyal is the doubt whether England would not prefer to see us out of the way—independent, annexed to the United States, anywhere, rather than a standing temptation to our friends. . . . At home, the argument *ab inconveniente* finds a ready acceptance with the masses, and when we find able pens arguing that all Colonial possessions are sources of national weakness, that this assertion, if true, is especially so of Canada, we may be excused for believing, or at least greatly fearing, that the declaration so frequently made of late, that we may go when we please, may very soon assume a different expression—that the hint to separate may be turned into the command to do so.

". . . Better, if we must separate from our Fatherland, that we swallow the bitter draught in its entirety, forego our British birthright, and, by annexation, secure at least safety either from assault or ridicule—any fate rather than assume the pitiful *rôle* of nationality on suffrance. . . . They know that the prospect of such a fate for our dominion is hateful to the loyal thousands of the country; but with very obvious craft, they take advantage of the utterances of the anti-Colonial party, and the policy of the Government, as expressed by Lord Granville, to tell us that independence is thrust upon us, and that either we must ask for a divorce, or England will pronounce the sentence without consulting our wishes.

"Again, a reference has been made to the loyalty of our people. It is not willingly that the subject is introduced; so constantly has our honest love to our country been sneered at by the so-called Liberal press of England, that we abstain from all mention of a feeling which, in the olden time at least, was always spoken of with honour. Yet, and in spite of the sneer at our old-fashioned faith, in spite of the cold water which such papers as the *Times* throw upon our professions, we do once more declare that love to England and to England's Queen is a principle so deeply felt in Canada, that the sentence which should condemn us to give up our allegiance would freeze the hearts of hundreds of thousands of Her Majesty's most faithful subjects.

SADDENING REFLECTIONS. 99

. . . If our countrymen in Britain could see and mark the kindling eyes, and hear the hearty cheers which greet every allusion to our Queen, or even the unfolding of our old honoured flag in the remotest of our villages, they would not join in the heartless taunt which says that our love is but regard for our pockets, or protestations from gratitude for favours—'to come.'

"Neither in our House of Commons nor in our newspapers are these questions thus far made subjects of much discussion. Talked of, of course, they are, but our future prospects do not yet form topics of vital interest, so far as public debate is concerned. In truth, in the midst of great material prosperity, our population increasing and thriving, everything looking bright, it is hard to notice signs which speak of changes which may be disastrous. We willingly shut our eyes to the handwriting on the wall; but in the hearts of the people, in private conversation among friends by the fireside, the question which is constantly agitated, which must soon be openly put and solemnly answered, is, 'Shall we act upon the ominous declaration of the home authorities—ominous because reiterated in season and out of season—that whenever we wish to separate from the Mother Country we are most welcome to do so? or shall we wait, hoping against hope, till this cold hint be changed to the colder command to—Go?'

"A CANADIAN."

Saddening reflections such as the above will call forth, occur to the readers of the article in the *Times* of the same date, headed " Great Britain and Australia."

THE AUTHOR OF "GINX'S BABY" ON IMPERIAL FEDERATION.

P.S.—January 3, 1871.—I have just received the *Contemporary Review* for this month, and read with singular pleasure the article on "*Imperial Federalism*," by the author of "Ginx's Baby." This eloquent and earnest appeal ought to be circulated widely,—if possible, in the form of a cheap pamphlet. By obliging permission of Messrs. Strahan, we are enabled to give the following clippings; but the whole requires to be read, in order to appreciate its vigour and force. Any one who looks at the several speeches and writings which mark the rapid growth and the strong set of popular opinion on this now developed subject of agitation, must be struck with their quite unconscious, but therefore most encouraging, accord even in language.

In connexion with the subject of a dear friend's pamphlet, mentioned on page 96, and with the subject of Emigration, reference is made to the article in another January monthly, "To what Extent is England Prosperous?" by Henry Fawcett, M.P.

"This is the period of Drift. Swept along by wind and current, our political and social tendencies appear to be escaping from our governance, and to be manœuvred by fate. It needs no deep mind to discover it. Capping leaded leaders in our daily papers, or suggesting to the "artists" of some of the many vulgar *comics*—O sad misnomer !— a subject of grotesque satire, the idea of Drifting is clearly recognized as a thing of the age. Drifting into war, drifting into a conference, drifting into danger, drifting into Church and State controversy, drifting to imperial dissolution—the term is now a favourite one to apply to our political movement—the tendency even seems to be favourably acquiesced in.

Drifting to Imperial Dissolution: I wish before heaven that I could lay hold and arrest the movement with a good, strong Samson's or Cromwell's hand! I cannot; but I have a voice, and I appeal from the politicians to the people of the Empire. Driftwood politicians; sweeping on before the breath of popularity—with no stern, proud principles to rule their motions—both parties of them eddying round and round here in a Reform whirlwind, tossed out of the way there by an Irish gust, spun about again by a German-French tempest, inanely watching the play of a Russian nor'-easter—*and liking it!* seeming contented with that lot, absolutely looking for the winds and currents as god-sends to be yielded to—glad if they blow hard enough to make it clear that it is the way they must go. I pray you, any sensible by-stander, any interested Briton, whose own and his children's fate is in the boat with these helmsmen; and even you, O captain and mates! do you call this statesmanship or farce?

Ought not these men to announce boldly in the face of us all: "This and this is our design—this is our best gospel in such and such a matter: there is the point we mean to try to reach, blow wind or run tide ever so strongly against us: if you don't approve of our intentions, they are honourable, and in all honesty don't expect *us* to carry out any other. Here we resign to any man who has another plan, if you think it a better one. *Our* scheme is true, we believe, and will hold on to be true, though the very foundations of the world were discovered; and till we can preach it fairly into your convictions, we shall cease to be responsible for the steering?" If we get not soon some such determined and specific-minded captains, brother-citizens, we are lost.

At this moment we are drifting to the disintegration of our Empire. Few believe it. Few have seen the great currents sweeping away off beyond the horizon, commencing their vast circuits even at the antipodes; but ere long the cyclone will burst upon us, and every one, especially the chief officers, will acknowledge a Divine wind, and calmly resign themselves to see the vessel rocked and blown to pieces, saving themselves, no doubt, "some on boards, and some on broken pieces of the ship. And so it came to pass that they——." I should like to know where our island of Melita will be, and whether the barbarians are likely to be civil. Meantime, I pray your earnest attention to the matters hereafter to be submitted, too conscious that my voice is weak in contest with the now boisterous elements of Drift, but having faith in my soul that these matters are serious and true. . . .

I define Imperial Federalism to be: The doctrine of a legislative union, in the form of a Confederation, of each subordinate self-governing community which is now included within the British Empire. To preserve that Empire intact, on the ground that such a policy is not only Imperial, but dictated by the selfish interest of each constituent; to combine in some flexible and comprehensive system the great concourse of subordinate States whereof our Empire is composed, for the benefit of all; and lastly, to confirm to every individual member of the Imperial Community those rights and privileges to which he is born —rights and privileges justly inalienable from himself or his children: these three things must be at once the aim and the reason for Imperial Federalism.

The gravity of the questions depending on this doctrine, every day pressing more urgently for solution, must ere long drive it to the front rank of political movement. What shall our Empire be fifty years hence? What shall become of those sons and daughters gone from our bosom to far-off territories, bearing with them a portion of our strength, our civilization, our freedom, our love of Motherland? Who are to be the legatees of the vastest national estate ever accumulated in one sovereign hand? Are our Colonies destined to be our weakness or our strength—to sap or to solidify our power? Is it the wisest policy to smooth the way to Imperial dissolution, or our duty and policy together, by every honest means, by every honourable bond, to perpetuate Imperial integrity? Are the hopes of unborn generations most engaged in the maintenance of an united Empire, or the development of separate nations? Such, and a hundred other questions, crop up in the hitherto unexplored regions of the subject designated by me Imperial Federalism. . . .

I have said that Federation exists already within the Queen's dominions. In 1856 the proposal to confederate the British North American Provinces is stated to have been regarded by Canadian statesmen "as visionary." In 1867 it was adopted throughout those vast provinces and by the Imperial Government. . . .

In the West Indies, Sir Benjamin Pyne has recently been able to induce several islands to unite upon a Confederation scheme, which will receive the sanction of the Home Government.

Following these accomplished facts, the principle of Federalism has naturally found its way to Australia, where, as we shall directly see, it has assumed a serious aspect. But the idea has not been allowed to float about and drop its seeds only on the extremities of the Empire. From them it has been borne home to ourselves, and has begun to germinate in Ireland. There, though perhaps fostered more by disaffection than the spirit of patriotism, it would yet be the most wanton prejudice to permit its infelicitous associations to distort our judgment of its political promises. It may, perhaps, hereafter be shown that some of the most urgent reasons for a federation of the Empire lie at home, and are not only to be sought in the necessities or the aspirations of our Colonial provinces. . . .

Turn where we will, we find Britain flourishing by the help of her own offspring—toiling, tilling, trading in and from her distant provinces. To every clime have her adventurous sons borne the civilization along with the enterprise of their race. Prairies and deserts have changed their features, and from their rich unnumbered acres has been brought the blessed food for millions at home. Nor this alone. The thoughtful workman here looks out with hopeful pride to communities of growing wealth and power, whose increasing necessities daily add to the demands for the products of his labour. They provide him with food, they provide him with staples of manufacture, they provide him with work, and they offer him, should he aim at higher things, the safest and most inviting field for his energies. To know that wherever he goes he still retains his English rights, still is safe under English protection, may at any time return and lie down to rest a citizen in his English home—is not this to make him feel the true value of an Imperial destiny? Is not this to give courage to the men and women who otherwise would perish here in the hopeless rivalry of wretchedness? Is not this a true, righteous, practical thing to devise and confirm for the good of every living soul within these crowded kingdoms?

What would not Germany give for such another Empire as Australia? What energy or money, or political and legislative zeal, or commercial enterprise, would she not lavish in establishing and riveting her relations with such a Colony? What a strength would she not draw from that young strong son? And we! . . .

It has of late years been the apparent policy of our Government, whether in Whig or Tory hands, to encourage independence in our greater provinces, especially independence of us in the matter of expense, this being most fatally the prime reason; a proper thing to encourage if it means a vigorous, self-reliant energy and life, but an ignoble and foolish policy if thereby is instigated a factious disavowal of Imperial relations. Yet the clumsy management of two or three Secretaries of State has nearly brought us to the latter point. But to give to each province the maximum of independent action, and yet preserve for it and for the Empire at large the maximum of mutual aid and benefit, is a problem that seems not to have occurred to, far less to have been attempted by, these summary statesmen. This is the exact problem which, I venture to affirm, Imperial Federalism alone can solve. . . .

An elaborate paper, contributed to the *New York Herald* of July

6th, and admitted by Canadian papers to be partly based on fact, contains some singular disclosures. Questionable as is the authority, the allegations are so specific and important as to demand attention. According to this statement, an Independence party have for some years been organizing treason in Canada. . . .

[Who will object to this manly word?]

Is it possible that much manœuvring of the Cabinet on Colonial questions was due to such tricksters—nay, are there any of them in the Colonial Office? This office seems to me, more than any department of State, to need a visit from a strong reformer with a good broom. Two or three times does the writer reiterate the allegations about co-conspirators in England. For instance:—

"On the day that Mr. Huntington and Mr. Young held their Waterloo meeting, *assurances were received from their friends in England that the Gladstone Cabinet could be depended upon to carry out the policy of independence.*"

Again:—

"In the fall of 1869 very positive assurances were forwarded to Canada *by friends who could speak semi-officially* that the English Administration had resolved on the following programme with regard to Canada:—1. The withdrawal of the Imperial forces. 2. The cessation of the system of Imperial guarantee. 3. The declaration of the independence of Canada at the earliest possible moment."

No one who has watched the details of our recent intercourse with the Dominion will be disposed to think the above statements improbable. I deem it my duty to insert them here that they may be distinctly contradicted if untrue. This looks like Drift again, only with a hope that Drift will be in a certain direction. We are exposed to the possibility of waking up unexpectedly to find our Empire slipped away in a night; cut loose by our statesmen. No indifferent reason for an immediate decision of the public upon the nature of our future policy.

The New Zealand case is too fresh in every one's mind to require that I should do more than refer to it. It proved by one example how delicate were the relations between ourselves and the whole of the Pacific Colonies. . . .

The Colony raised its own forces and repressed the insurrection, but it bitterly resented the cold inflexibility of the English Cabinet, not less than Lord Granville's recommendation to acknowledge within the Queen's dominions the sovereignty of a Maori chief! Some of the first men of the Colony began to look, as its only hope, to junction with the United States, who were certain to supply necessary forces to defend any member of their confederacy. The Imperial Government was successfully threatened with the alternative of help or secession. Under the fear and pressure of public opinion at home, Lord Granville yielded only at the latest hour before the fatal telegram was to have been sent to the New Zealand Government.

Within the last month significant news has reached this country from Australia. . . .

When the disintegration of our Empire is recommended by a Royal Commission,* it is time to consider whether Her Majesty is to be Queen only of Great Britain or an Imperial Sovereign. The proposal of the Victoria statesmen is unpractical. Such a relation of independent "sovereignties" could not be maintained in this age, and we have seen even in democratic America how the attempt to assert State sovereignty against confederated power was stifled in blood. The Australians will look to one or other of the great leading Powers of the Anglo-Saxon race; and a continuance of our repulsive policy will drive them, not to independence, but to the United States. The quaint warning of an American diplomatist to a political friend of mine is not so exaggerated as might be supposed : " *The United States is watching, and I guess she'll pick up everything you let drop.*" Not another nation under heaven is so suicidally regardless of the pillars of its power.

Before such schemes are further elaborated, may not we and the Australian Colonies judiciously consider what claims the Imperial Government, representing the British nation, has upon those provinces ? Colonial Ministers acting under the Crown have from time to time constituted small patches of society, excised from our own community, the absolute owners of property held, in all moral and political honesty, in trust for the people and Government of these islands; for it was won and maintained by our adventure and sacrifice. A slip of an Imperial pen has unreservedly transferred whole provinces to those casual communities; but this has been done with the implied trust that they should be held and used only in harmony with Imperial interests. No Minister or Government had the power to confer more. These territories, from which we might have drawn Imperial revenues, are now administered solely in the interest of the settlers. We exact from them

---

* I copy the First Report *in extenso*, from the *Launceston Examiner* of Nov. 5, at the end of these clippings.

no direct pecuniary profit. They have been the gift by which we meant to reward the enterprise of our adventurous sons. But they must not suppose that they have the right to divest them of the Imperial *dominium*. They hold them as our fellow-citizens, on the basis of their citizenship, and against the Imperial will they cannot assume the right of removing them from our sovereignty. Every man, woman, and child in these islands has a right and voice in the future position of our Colonies; the sooner they and we understand it the better for all. The " unwashed " millions may claim their interest in the matter, and insist that careless statesmanship and intemperate politics shall not jeopardise the enormous stake they have in the integrity of our dominions.

If anybody should represent that in permitting our Colonies to separate from us we and they should be fulfilling our destiny, my retort is that destiny appears very much to be under the control of men: within certain limits our destiny is what we make it. . . .

How much we have to gain in time of peace by the consolidation of Imperial connexions it is needless here at any length to recall. The arguments used in support of emigration—the proofs adduced of mutual profit from intercourse and trade—are only strengthened when we consider their bearing under a more organized and complete union. Should a federal system be devised, whereby every Colony has its rightful place and representation in the Imperial connexion, whereby to every Colonist was assured Imperial citizenship, with all its resultant rights of protection and freedom, it is impossible but that the ideal distinctions between " Home " and " the Colonies " would vanish away. Instead of hearing ignorant men among the uninstructed classes, and unwise men among the instructed classes, speak of an emigrant as " an exile," and our birthright estates beyond the seas as " foreign lands,' we should know no difference between England, Scotland, Ireland, Canada, and Australia, except the divisions of space, and no boundary of " Home " other than the limits of our Empire. . . .

The timidity of wealth, as well as that of thinking labour and personality, to which I have already alluded, partly arises from the uncertainty of our relations to our Colonies, which, along with considerable ignorance regarding the Colonies themselves, makes the capitalist hesitate to trust his money in Colonial enterprises. If Canada is likely to become independent, if New Zealand is any day to go off in a pet, who can foresee what the value of their securities, or their railways, or their public works or private speculations will be? But confirmed in federal union, with ultimate resort to federal courts, with more constant intercourse and a permanent official representation at the Imperial capital—with the whole system of our English business expanded, its banks, trades, companies, agencies, communicating and acting together within the Empire as they now do within Great Britain—we foresee in Federalism a promise of development for our wealth hitherto unconceived by the most dreamy worshipper of Plutus. And the possibility has been concluded by the steam and telegraph, which have destroyed the obstacles of distance. The Colonies also would gain their advantage from the new relation, in the ready inflow of capital for all purposes of development.

Not only in this way would the wealth of the Empire be quickened into more general circulation, but from the Imperial point of view Federalism promises to settle in the happiest way the difficulties arising through the unequal incidence of the burthens of Imperial expense. I do not here advert to the National Debt—a subject which would need special arrangements under any system of federation. One of the prime conditions of federation would be that the charges in matters of common interest should be equally borne, those of more immediate concern to any member of the confederacy being left to the adjudication of its local Government. Under this arrangement Englishmen in England could no longer complain that they were unfairly taxed for the benefit of Englishmen in America, or Africa, or Australia; for even granting that at any period any single member of the confederacy should need peculiar assistance, its constant contribution to the Imperial exchequer would in the end more than outweigh the temporary obligation. . . .

Measures of Imperial, national, or Colonial importance are hustled out of the way by one or two, sometimes, of secondary consequence, which have happened to engage popular sympathies. Here is the secret of Ministerial worship of Drift. Some of the most crying evils of the day retain their vicious power, some of the most needful reforms are unaccomplished, because there are limits to legislative time and human endurance. If this pressure continues in anything like the present ratio of increase, the Empire must perish of congestion of the brain. . . .

It is worth while to observe the discrepancy between the numbers arising out of the three kingdoms. The proportion of English statutes is too largely in excess of those from Scotland and Ireland to be accounted for simply by the disproportion of population, wealth, and prosperity. It must be taken that from either of the lesser provinces there would, in the event of greater legislative facilities, be more legislation, and the activity of legislation is a better sign for a country than its inertness. Conversely, I assume that the deficiency of legislation of the kind here under discussion, for two countries like Scotland and Ireland, is, in part, fairly attributable to a deficiency of facilities for accomplishing it.

Those Acts of a quasi-imperial character termed "Public and General Statutes," yield the following results, allowing to the description Imperial the widest scope :—

Imperial statutes—*e.g.*, Army, Navy, Revenue, &c., &c.		45
Technical statutes — amending laws or affecting legal questions, &c. (these might be either local or Imperial)		15
Local statutes :—England	26	
,, Ireland	16	
,, Scotland	7	
,, India	2	
,, England and Ireland	1	
		— 52
Total		112

Hence, had there existed an Imperial Parliament and separate local Governments in England, Scotland, and Ireland, less than one-half of the Public General Statutes would have come within the province of Imperial legislation—that is, 45 out of 97.

The result upon the whole legislation is, that out of 293 Acts there were—

Imperial	48
Technical	15
English	166
Irish	35
Scotch	26
Indian	2
England and Ireland together ...	1
Total	293

Less than *one-sixth* in number of all the Acts of last session could be characterized as Imperial; the rest were properly referable to the localities immediately affected by them.* . . .

An office, presided over by a shifting partizan, however able, however honest, however industrious—actually conducted by a permanent staff, seldom, if ever, selected for any reputation of experience in colonial life—an office, to visit which is for a Colonist like reconnoitring an enemy — to negotiate with which is like a war parley, and to assault which needs almost a forlorn hope and a battery—is, spite of any brilliant abilities existing in it, incapable of discharging with success the infinitely varied, numerous, delicate, and detailed duties essential to its business. To every Colony, each with its own wrongs or rights or difficulties, such an office is sure to appear unwise or tyrannical, because, in its very constitution, its aspect is to them *foreign*. Their delegates do not meet officials from their own colony—they meet bigoted domestic Englishmen. Not infrequently, before they can open a negotiation, or even make a statement, they are obliged to give imperfect instruction in the conditions of the people or places to be the subject of official attention. This cannot continue long. The Colonies must have better audience at Whitehall, or they will have done knocking at our doors. . . .

A senate or parliament of representatives from every province, deliberating in public, and acting on the decision of the majority, would of necessity satisfy all the objections to the present system. All other schemes, such as that of a representative Colonial Council, Colonist Ministers, limited representation in the Imperial Parliament, and so forth, dwindle before the practical simplicity of federal union. . . .

---

* I had myself made a similar analysis for the Sessions 1869 and 1870. It was not made with great nicety, but is sufficiently accurate, and *apropos* to subjoin:—

Acts.	1869.	1870.
England	49	35
Ireland	10	16
England and Ireland	8	5
United Kingdom	34	38
Man, &c.	0	4
India	9	3
Colonies	4	3
	117	112
Private Acts	171	181
	288	293

Nothing need be added to prove that the Federal principle is capable of embodiment in a form at once promoting unity, protecting personal liberty, and fostering local independence, while in enlarging the scope of Imperial splendour it gives strength to the play of Imperial loyalty.

I have sought simply to preach the doctrine of Federalism, not to indicate the method of Federation. Without pretence of exhaustive treatment, enough has, I hope, been said to prove the desirability of inquiring throughout our Empire whether Federation be feasible or impossible. It is likely that I shall be met with the familiar sneer that I have dreamed a magnificent dream. Had Bismarck ten years ago dreamed aloud the actual happenings of these wondrous and terrible days, would he not have been consigned to some careful asylum?"

FIRST REPORT OF THE ROYAL COMMISSION APPOINTED BY THE VICTORIA GOVERNMENT.

As this unpleasant, though courteous, document is of great national interest and importance, I produce it here *in extenso*. I put part into italics, chiefly with a view to call attention to truths grievously misapplied :—

'To His Excellency the Right Hon. John Henry Thomas Viscount Canterbury, K.C.B., Governor and Commander-in-Chief of the Colony of Victoria.

"We, the undersigned Commissioners appointed under Letters Patent from the Crown, bearing date the 31st day of August, 1870, to consider and report upon the necessity of a Federal Union of the Australian Colonies for Legislative purposes, and the best means of accomplishing such a union, beg to submit to your Excellency this our first Report :—

" 1. The two questions referred to the Commission have been carefully and separately considered.

" I.—Advantages of a Federal Union.

"2. On the primary question of a Federal Union of the Australian Colonies, apart from all considerations of the time and method of bringing such a union about, there was a unanimity of opinion. The indispensable condition of success for men or nations is, that they should clearly understand what they want, and to what goal they were travelling, that life may not be wasted in doing and undoing ; and as we are persuaded that the prosperity and security of these Colonies would be effectually promoted by enabling them to act together as one people under the authority of a federal compact, they cannot, we believe, too soon come to an understanding upon this fundamental point.

" 3. The difference in strength and *prestige* between isolated communities having separate interests and a *National Confederation with a national policy*, has been illustrated in the history of almost every great State in the world, and conspicuously in the history of *States of which we share the blood and traditions*. The effects of such a Confederation, when it is voluntary and equal, are felt throughout all the complicated relations of a nation's life, adding immensely to its material and moral strength. By its concentrated power it exercises an increased gravitation in *attracting population and commerce*. It multiplies the national wealth by putting an end to jealous and wasteful competitions, and substituting the wise economy of power which teaches each district to apply itself to the industries in which it can attain the greatest success. *It enlarges the home market, which is the nursing mother of native manufactures.* It forms larger designs, engages in larger enterprises, and by its increased resources and authority causes them to be more speedily accomplished. It obtains additional security for peace by increasing its means of defence; and, *by creating a nation, it creates along with it a sentiment of nationality*—a sentiment which has been one of the strongest and most beneficent motive powers in human affairs. The method, indeed, by which States have grown great is almost uniform in history: *they gathered population and territory, and on these wings rose to material power;* and *with the sense of a common citizenship there speedily came*, like a soul to the inert body, *that public spirit by whose inspiration dangers are willingly faced* and privations cheerfully borne in the sacred name of country.

"4. We cannot doubt that it is the destiny of the Australian Colonies to *pursue a similar career, and their duty to prepare for it*. They possess resources and territory which *fit them to become in the end a great Empire;* they are occupied by a population already larger than the population of many sovereign States, and they yield a revenue greater than the revenue of six of the Kingdoms of Europe; and we believe they share the sentiments, which may be noted as among the most subtile and pervading influences of our century, the desire to *perfect the union and autonomy of peoples of the same origin.*

"II.—BEST MEANS OF EFFECTING A UNION.

"5. The form which a Federal Union ought to assume, and the time at which it ought to be brought into operation, are subjects which must be reserved for a Conference of Colonial Delegates accredited by the respective Governments and Legislatures concerned.

"6. In approaching the second question referred to us, however— the best means of effecting a union—it is necessary to point out that a federal compact for Legislative purposes may represent widely different ideas and measures of power. The Canadian Dominion furnishes the most perfect example of Federated Colonies. Canada, Nova Scotia, New Brunswick, and Prince Edward's Island enjoyed constitutions substantially the same as ours, and were, consequently, under the control of Governments responsible only to the local Legislatures. For the purpose of attaining the increased vigour and authority which result from union, these Colonies agreed to abandon some of the powers enjoyed by the local Legislatures in favour of a general Parliament and Government authorized to act on behalf of all the Confederated Colonies. A constitution was framed accordingly, under which each Colony retains a local Legislature, possessing complete control over purely local interests, and over the public lands of the Colony, while the Parliament and the Executive of the Dominion are charged with what may be distinguished as national interests. We have printed in an Appendix the principal clauses of the Act of the Imperial Parliament creating the Dominion of Canada, from which the functions of the local and general Legislatures respectively may be seen in detail. On the other hand, there have been examples of a Federal Council having authority only on a few specified subjects, and on such other subjects as were afterwards from time to time referred to it by the local Legislatures. And there have been intermediate methods of more or less perfectly organized union. Opinion in the Colonies seems to be divided between these methods; and a decision can only be arrived at after much debate and negotiation.

"7. But there is a preliminary work to be done, upon which there would probably be a little difference of opinion. To effect a union of any kind, binding alike upon all, an Imperial Act is necessary. Such an Act might be a permissive one, and might authorize the Queen, by proclamation, to call into existence a Federal Union of any two or more of the Australian Colonies as soon as they passed Acts in their respective Legislatures providing, in identical terms, for the powers and functions to be exercised by the General Legislature, and the distribution of seats, and for the adjustment of the Colonial debts in case the nature of the union should render an adjustment necessary. The bases of these identical Acts would, of course, be determined by Conference between the Colonies.

"8. The Permissive Act ought to provide for the admission of Colonies not joining the Union in the first instance, and might also provide a mode of withdrawal upon certain notice for any Colony dissatisfied.

"9. We are distinctly of opinion that 'the best means of accomplishing a union' is to remove, by such an act, all legal impediments to it without delay, and leave the Colonies to determine, by negotiation among themselves, how far, and how soon, they will avail themselves of the power thus conferred on them.

"10. The Commission are disposed to regard it as part of *the duty committed to them to prepare a bill for transmission to the Imperial Parliament* of the nature which they have indicated, and to ascertain by communication with the leading public men in the other Colonies whether they are disposed to co-operate in securing the sanction of the Imperial Parliament for it. While all questions of Intercolonial relations must be reserved for a Colonial Conference, it seems plain that, unless those who make a proposal of this nature give it practical shape and take means to ascertain how far it will be acceptable, it may prove as barren of results as many proposals on the same subject which have preceded it. *They intend, therefore, to print such a bill with their second Report.*

"III.—THE NEUTRALITY OF THE COLONIES IN WAR.

"11. A cognate question has been brought under the consideration of the Commission, as belonging to its general object—the existing relation of the Colonies to each other and to the Mother Country.

"12. *The British Colonies from which Imperial troops have been wholly withdrawn present the unprecedented phenomenon of responsibility without either corresponding authority or adequate protection.* They are as liable to all the hazards of war as the United Kingdom; but *they can influence the commencement or continuance of war no more than they can control the movements of the solar system;* and they have no certain assurance of that aid against an enemy upon which integral portions of the United Kingdom can confidently reckon. This is *a relation so wanting in mutuality that it cannot safely be regarded as a lasting one,* and it becomes necessary to consider how it may be so modified as to afford a *greater security for permanence.*

"13. It has been proposed to establish *a Council of the Empire, whose advice must be taken before war was declared.* But this measure is so *foreign* to the genius and traditions of the British Constitution, and presupposes so large an abandonment of its functions by the House of Commons, *that we dismiss it from consideration.* There remains, however, we think, more than one method by which the anomaly of the present system may be cured.

"14. It is a maxim of international law, that a *sovereign State* cannot be involved in war without its own consent, and that *while two or more*

States are subject to the same Crown, and allies in peace, they are not, therefore, necessarily associates in war if the one is *not dependent on the other.*

"15. *The sovereignty of a State does not arise from its extent, or power, or population,* or form of government. More than a century ago Vattel formulated the principle now universally accepted, that a small community may be a sovereign State no less than the most powerful Kingdom or Empire, and that all sovereign States inherit the same rights and obligations.

"16. 'Two sovereign States,' says Vattel, 'may be subject to the same prince without any dependence on each other, and each may retain its rights as a free and sovereign State. The King of Prussia is Sovereign Prince of Neufchatel in Switzerland, without the principality being in any manner united to his other dominions; so that the people of Neufchatel, in virtue of their franchises, may serve a foreign Power at war with the King of Prussia, provided that the war be not on account of that principality.'

"17. Wheaton and other modern public jurists have illustrated the same principle by the case of Hanover and England, which, though they were allied by personal union under the same Crown, were not necessarily associates in war, or responsible for each other. And the latest writers on international law cite the more modern and analogous case of the Ionian Islands, a State garrisoned by British troops, and having as chief magistrate a Lord High Commissioner appointed by the Queen, and which was, notwithstanding, adjudged before the British Court of Admiralty (on a private question arising) to constitute a sovereign State not associated with the United Kingdom in the Crimean War. The last chief magistrate but one of this sovereign State was since promoted to the Governorship of the Colony of New South Wales, and thence to the Governorship of the domain of Canada. The last Lord High Commissioner was transferred to the Governorship of the Dependency of Jamaica.

"18. Without overlooking the distinction between Colonies consisting of men of the same origin as the population of the United Kingdom, and States inherited by the Crown, like Hanover, or obtained by treaty, like the Ionian Islands, it is suggested for consideration whether the rule of international law under which they are declared neutrals in war would not become applicable to Colonies enjoying self-government by a single addition to their present power.

"19. The Colony of Victoria, for example, possesses a separate Parliament, Government, and *distinguishing flag ; a separate naval and military establishment.* All the public appointments are made by the local Government. The only officer commissioned from England who exercises authority within its limits is the Queen's representative; and in the Ionian Islands, while they were admittedly a sovereign State, the Queen's representative was appointed in the same manner. The single function of a sovereign State, as understood in international law, which the Colony does not exercise or possess, is *the power of contracting obligations with other States. The want of this power alone distinguishes her position from that of States undoubtedly sovereign.*

"20. If the Queen were authorized by the Imperial Parliament to concede to the greater Colonies the right to make treaties, it is contended that they would fulfil the conditions constituting a sovereign State in as full and perfect a sense as any of the smaller States cited by public jurists to illustrate this rule of limited responsibility. And the notable concession to the interests of peace and humanity made in our own day by the *Great Powers* with respect to privateers and to merchant shipping renders it probable that they *would not,* on any inadequate grounds, *refuse to recognize* such States as falling under the rule.

"21. It must not be forgotten that this is a subject in which *the interests of the Colonies and of the Mother Country are identical.* British statesmen have long aimed not only to limit more and more the expenditure incurred for the defence of distant Colonies, but to withdraw more and more from all ostensible responsibility for their defence; and they would probably see *any* honourable method of *adjusting the present anomalous relations* with no less satisfaction than we should.

"22. Nor would the recognition of the neutrality of the self-governed Colonies deprive them of the power of aiding the Mother Country in any *just and neccesary* war. On the contrary, it would enable them to *aid her with more dignity* and effect; as a sovereign State could *of its own free will,* and, *at whatever period it thought proper,* elect to become a party to the war.

"23. We are of opinion that *this subject ought to be brought under the notice of the Imperial Government.* If the proposal should receive their sanction, they can ascertain the wishes of the *American and African Colonies* with respect to it, and finally take the necessary measures to obtain its recognition as part of the public law of the civilized world.

    (l.s.) C. GAVAN DUFFY, Chairman.
    ,, FRANCIS MURPHY.
    ,, THO. HOWARD FELLOWS.
       (As to Parts I. and II.)
    ,, C. M'MAHON.
    ,, JOHN MACGREGOR.
    ,, J. F. SULLIVAN.
    ,, EDWARD LANGTON.
       (Except as to Part III.)
    ,, J. J. CASEY.
    ,, G. B. KERFERD.
    ,, GRAHAM BERRY.
    ,, JAS. GRAHAM."

"Town Hall, Melbourne, October 3, 1870.

INDEX.

	PAGE
Act 18 and 19 Vic., c. 54	81
AFRICAN Colonies ... vii, 41, 66,	117
Aggregative Tendency of the Age	19, 85
Agriculture's Advantages to a Nation compared with Export Trades 6, 32,	96
Alienizing ... ... iv, 4,	92
Allegiance 63,	74
Anti-Immigration League ...	79
Armaments ... 27, 36, 52, 76,	97
"Atlantica"	25
AUSTRALIA 19, 22, 41, 57, 67, 70, 71, 73, 78, 79, 80, 82, 93, 99, 106,	117
,, Royal Commission 50, 106,	112
,, Conference ... 19, 42,	58
,, Emigrants to	87
Bacon, Lord	62
Bentham, Jeremy	72
Board, A Colonial ... 11, 16,	56
BOMBAY	54
Butler, General	vi
CANADA ... viii, 4, 18, 41, 50, 51, 53, 67, 77, 95, 97, 103, 105,	113
CAPE Route	vii
Capital 10,	107
Carlyle	73
"Cavete canes" 25,	43
CELTIC Element 2,	25
Citizenship	4
Coaling Stations	54
Colomb, Captain	52
Colonial Office 10, 15, 27, 82,	110
Colonial Questions ... ... v,	95
Colonies are Co-Partners ... 13,	64
,, Benefits they confer 73, 75,	94
,, Benefits they receive 9, 35, 76,	94
,, Claim of vi, 14, 43, 46,	50
,, Cost of	77
,, Equalizing with Mother Country ... 12, 34,	65
,, Expectations from ... iii,	37
,, Fears of ... 18, 49,	98
,, Improved Administration of	63
,, Loyalty of the 18, 33, 45,	98
,, Neutrality of	115
,, Parties in the	93
,, Representation in Cabinet ...	16
,, "Tributary States" ...	81
Colonisation 58, 68, 70,	72
,, Object	61
,, GREEK 68,	70
,, ROMAN	69
,, UNITED STATES ...	69
Colonists, How Welcomed ... 10,	110
,, in LONDON ... 38,	84
"Colony" Defined	60

	PAGE
COLUMBIA, British ...	51
"Coming Event, The," by Dr. Lang	48
Commission at MELBOURNE ...	50
Conference at MELBOURNE 19, 42,	58
Contemporary Review	101
Crown Rights	80
Council of the Empire 16, 40, 84,	85
Daily Review	97
Debt, National 31, 35, 36, 75, 92,	108
Defence of Colonies vii, 19, 46, 52,	83
Dismemberment ... 21, 47, 66,	101
Disloyalty 63, 105, 106,	113
Dominance 65,	76
"Drifting" 101,	108
Edinburgh Review	48
Emigration ... iv, 10, 23, 33, 78, 80, 82, 87, 91, 94, 101	107
,, Fund for ... 78, 81,	89
,, Report on	87
"Empire" Defined	1
,, Unification 35, 56,	70
,, Council of the ... 16,	28
,, Integrity of the 34, 41,	48
,, too Extensive"	66
,, Weal of, True Policy 2,	33
ENGLAND, Love Towards ... 50,	65
ENGLISH Emigrants	87
Fawcett, Professor, M.P.	101
Federation 16, 43,	56
,, Australian 42, 83, 84, 103,	112
,, Canadian	103
,, West Indian	103
,, of Empire viii, 43, 65, 70, 84,	101
,, of English-speaking Countries	78
FIJI 58,	59
Foreign Emigrants	87
Fortresses 9,	18
FRANCE ... 9, 10, 19, 22, 23, 25, 43,	72
,, Colonies of	72
Franklin, Benjamin	72
Free Trade 9, 21, 33,	94
"Friends in Council," Author of ...	56
Froude, Mr.	82
Future, The 10, 25,	96
GAMBIA	vii
Gazette, British Columbia ...	51
GERMANY 9, 10, 19, 25, 30, 43, 60, 85,	104
Ginx's Baby, Author of ...	101
Gladstone, Right Hon. W. E. vii, 47, 93	105
GLASGOW, State of, and a Warning from	66
Good Words	56
Government, The ... 18, 41, 47,	67

INDEX.

	PAGE		PAGE
Granville, Earl ... 41, 97, 98,	106	Policy, Mistakes in 7, 32, 35, 38, 68,	102
Great Nations ... ... iii, 19,	85	Poor, their Interests Neglected 38,	
Grey, Earl 75,	84		66, 107
Grotius	71	Population ... 9, 24, 30, 35, 43,	78
Hansard ... ... v,	85	Popular Opinion ... 68, 85,	104
Helps, Arthur, Mr.	56	Protection, Adverse in Colonies ...	iii
Honours 12,	39	Quarterly Review	50
"Imperial," The Word	40	QUEENSLAND 41,	90
Improved Administration of Colonies	63	Roebuck, Mr.	70
Independence ... viii, 14, 19, 42, 43,		Royalty, its Opportunities	11
48, 50, 57, 63, 70, 93,	104	Russell, Earl	81
INDIA 20, 22,	85	RUSSIA ... 9, 20, 22, 23, 25, 30,	43
Institute, Royal Colonial	93	Sandon, Lord, M.P.	85
IONIAN ISLANDS	116	SCOTCH Emigrants	87
IRISH Emigrants	87	Secretary and Under-Secretary of	
Ireland, Legislation for	viii	State for the Colonies ...	47
Isolation of Portions of the Empire		Separation 17, 42, 46, 49, 5', 66,	
20,	30	74, 75, 83, 93,	113
Johnston, Rev. Jas., Glasgow ...	96	,, Loss to United Kingdom	
Land at Home	iv	by	84
,, Exchanging British for Colonial	39	Smith, Adam 71,	76
,, Grants Among ROMANS ...	69	Social Science Association ... 1,	20
,, ,, Requisite to Attract		SOUTH AUSTRALIA	89
Immigrants	79	"Sovereign State," A	115
,, Sales, &c., Revenue from ...	89	Steamships for Emigrants	86
,, South Australian	89	Strength, National, Whence 19,	30
,, Transfer to Colonies	3	Supply and Demand	8
,, Condition Implied ... 3,	44	Tariffs, Hostile	5
,, Waste 23, 32, 38, 70, 78, 80,	82	Times, The ... 45, 52, 67, 68, 93,	99
,, ,, Return, Parliamentary	79	Trade, Evils and Crises ... 5,	96
LANG, Rev. Dr. ... viii, 48,	57	,, Its Instability	5
LEITH	iv	,, with the Colonies ...22, 77,	94
Leith Herald	iii	,, Undue Favour for Export ...	vi
Lewis, Sir George	76	,, Value of Home ... 5,	112
LIVERPOOL as an Emigration Port iv,	69	"Treason"	105
M'Culloch's Dictionary of Commerce	69	Troops, Withdrawal of 8, 50, 59, 67,	115
Manchester, Duke of	84	UNITED KINGDOM, Duties of 26,	35
Melbourne Age	46	,, Place of 24, 75, 85,	95
Melbourne Argus	45	,, "Pride" of 33,	66
Merivale, Mr.	73	,, Rights of 38,	73
Misleading Impressions 18, 34, 53, 67,	94	,, Rule of, Generous	3
Montreal Gazette	46	,, Self-indulgence ...	31
Mortality in Steamships	88	,, Wishes ... 58,	59
"Mother Country"	34	UNITED STATES 9, 10, 20, 23, 24,	
Monsell, Right Hon. Wm., M.P. ...	47	30, 33, 36, 43, 56, 60,	
"Mutuality Awanting"	115	83, 95, 98, 106,	113
National Spirit ... ix, 10,	112	,, Colonisation 69,	71
Nationality 63, 85,	112	,, Congress	72
,, Australian ... 58,	65	,, Emigration to 77,	87
Negotiations 27, 49, 55,	80	,, Facilities there ...	4
NEUFCHATEL	116	,, National Spirit ...	10
NEW SOUTH WALES Land Sales ...	89	,, Relations with ...	24
,, ,, Constitution	80	,, their Separation a	
New York Herald	104	National Loss ...	77
NEW ZEALAND 49, 59, 66, 67, 97,	105	Value of Emigrants ... ... iv,	91
Nobility, their Duties ... 11,	39	Vattel	116
NOVA SCOTIA	iv	VICTORIA Commission v, 50, 106,	112
Northcote, Sir Stafford, M.P. ...	84	Wakefield, Mr. 65, 75,	78
Ocean Highways 46,	53	War ... 21, 31, 45, 49, 50, 78,	82
Pall Mall Gazette	50	Wellington Independent	49
Parliament v, 14, 15, 17, 27, 36,		Westgarth, Mr.	93
37, 42, 108,	115	Wodehouse, Sir Philip	86
Parnell, Sir Henry	77	Working Classes 4,	85
Party Question, Colonial is not 1,	47	Youl, J. A.	84
Pauperism, its Increase	99		

LONDON: W. J. JOHNSON, PRINTER, 121, FLEET STREET, E.C.

www.ingramcontent.com/pod-product-compliance
Lightning Source LLC
Chambersburg PA
CBHW020058170426
43199CB00009B/329